PENGUIN B

MAYBE
TOMORROW

'Many Australians wonder what life is really like for Aboriginals who live in two worlds. In *Maybe Tomorrow*, Boori Pryor tells us in a simple, story-telling way. He shares his hope without sparing us the pain or the history. In this book, you can hear him, feel the pain sharply, and gently touch the hope. Maybe tomorrow is sooner than we think.'

Father Frank Brennan

'I loved this timely book. *Maybe Tomorrow* is warm, gutsy, full of life. A tale of triumph over tragedy, amazingly free of judgement . . . highly recommended.' *Peter Garrett, Midnight Oil*

'This book provides a fascinating insight into the struggles that confront our people. More import-antly, it is a reflection of the barriers that Boori Pryor has overcome to deliver his message of reconciliation, respect and tolerance. I admire the commitment and vision demonstrated in this book.'

Gatjil Djerrkura, Chairman of ATSIC
(Aboriginal and Torres Strait Islander Commission)

Other books by Meme McDonald

Put Your Whole Self In
The Way of the Birds

Sue   2000

From across the seas
with love and hope

Meme

MAYBE TOMORROW

BOORI (MONTY) PRYOR

with Meme McDonald

Photographs by
Meme McDonald

Illustrations by
Lillian Fourmile

PENGUIN BOOKS

Penguin Books Australia Ltd
487 Maroondah Highway, PO Box 257
Ringwood, Victoria 3134, Australia
Penguin Books Ltd
Harmondsworth, Middlesex, England
Penguin Putnam Inc.
375 Hudson Street, New York, New York 10014, USA
Penguin Books Canada Limited
10 Alcorn Avenue, Toronto, Ontario, Canada M4V 3B2
Penguin Books (N.Z.) Ltd
Cnr Rosedale and Airborne Roads, Albany, New Zealand
Penguin Books (South Africa) (Pty) Ltd
5 Watkins St, Denver Ext 4, 2094, South Africa
Penguin Books India (P) Ltd
11, Community Centre, Panchsheel Park
New Delhi 110 017, India

First published by Penguin Books Australia, 1998
7 9 11 13 12 10 8
Copyright © Boori (Monty) Pryor, Meme McDonald, Margaret Dunkle, 1998
Photographs copyright © Meme McDonald, 1998
Illustrations copyright © Lillian Fourmile, 1998

Consulting Editor, Margaret Dunkle
Designed by Jo Hunt, Penguin Design Studio
Maps by Cathy Larsen
Typeset in 10½/15½ pt Garamond by Post Pre-press Group, Brisbane
Made and printed in Australia by Australian Print Group, Maryborough, Victoria

National Library of Australia
Cataloguing-in-Publication data:

Pryor, Boori, 1950– .
Maybe tommorow

ISBN 0 14 027397 2

1. Pryor, Boori, 1950– . 2. Pryor, Boori, 1950–
– childhood and youth. 3. Entertainers –
Australia – Biography. 4. Aborigines,
Australian – Biography. I. McDonald,
Meme, 1954– . II. Title.

791.092

Meme McDonald gratefully acknowledges the support of the Australia Council in
granting her a Fellowship from the Community Cultural Development Fund.

When the first edition of *Maybe Tomorrow* went to press, page 52 referred to Palm Island as the
land of the Wulgurukabba people. While this was thought to be correct at the time, it is now
recognised that this land belongs to the Munburra people.

On the cover of this book are the faces of four people very special to me. From left to right, they are my brother Nicky, Budda Paul, my sister Kimmy, and my nephew Liam. I dedicate this book to each of them and hope their voices can be heard through the words written. I know they were with me every step of the way, giving me the strength to look deep inside my heart to find forgiveness, in turn making me a much better human being. From that new place in my heart, I thank them.

BOORI (MONTY) PRYOR

CONTENTS

AUSTRALIA

DARWIN
Roper River
Kimberley
NT
Alice Springs
Finke R.
Uluru
WA
SA
Lake Eyre
PERTH
Cairns
Townsville
Burdekin River
Mackay
Rockhampton
QLD
BRISBANE
Armidale
Blue Mts
Kariong
NSW
Wagga Wagga
SYDNEY
CANBERRA
Bendigo
VIC
MELBOURNE
ADELAIDE
Point Cook
TAS
HOBART

QUEENSLAND

Laura
Cape Grafton
Kuranda
Mareeba
Cairns
Atherton Tableland
Yarrabah
Lucinda Point
Palm Island
Ingham
Townsville
Bohle River
Ross River
Ayr
Bowen
Mackay
Winton
Rockhampton
Cherbourg
BRISBANE

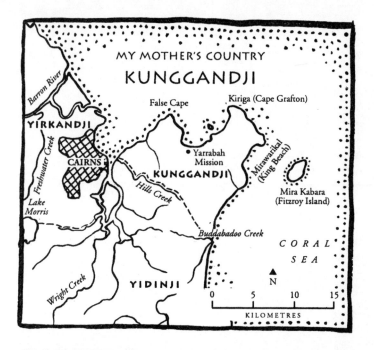

MY MOTHER'S COUNTRY
KUNGGANDJI

YIRKANDJI

CAIRNS

False Cape

Kiriga (Cape Grafton)

Yarrabah Mission

KUNGGANDJI

Mirawarikal (King Beach)

Mira Kabara (Fitzroy Island)

Barron River

Freshwater Creek

Lake Morris

Hills Creek

Buddabadoo Creek

Wright Creek

YIDINJI

CORAL SEA

N

0   5   10   15

KILOMETRES

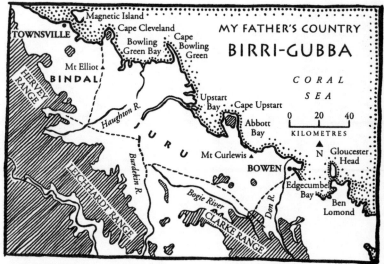

Magnetic Island

TOWNSVILLE

Cape Cleveland

Bowling Green Bay

Cape Bowling Green

MY FATHER'S COUNTRY
BIRRI-GUBBA

HERVEY RANGE

Mt Elliot

BINDAL

Haughton R.

Burdekin R.

U R U

Upstart Bay

Cape Upstart

Abbott Bay

CORAL SEA

0   20   40

KILOMETRES

Mt Curlewis

N

Gloucester Head

BOWEN

Edgecumbe Bay

Ben Lomond

LEICHHARDT RANGE

Bogie River

Don R.

CLARKE RANGE

--- indicates tribal boundaries

(These tribal boundaries are only approximate and are still under negotiation.)

This is my way of fighting.
The old people used to fight in a different way.
They fought with spears.
Then my parents fought to stay alive on the reserves.
The trick is to find your own style of fighting.
My brother just bent under the numbers.
He took everyone on at once and lost.
I'm fighting in a different way.
And I'm surviving.

Yarrabah

Yarrabah has always been my strength. It is where my mother's people are from.

1

WHAT I'M TALKING ABOUT

To feel happy about yourself you must feel
happy about the place you live in.

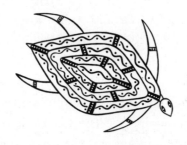

In 1982 I lost my brother. His name was Kenneth. We called him Nick. He was a beautiful, strong, young man. Although he was really skinny, he could go, he could fight with the best of them. When he hit, they stayed hit. He tried his best to fit into the white society but found it hard to relate to a city way of living. Whenever we went bush he was always a different person. He was at home in the bush. He used to go down the beach all the time. That was his special place. The Bohle. At the mouth of the Bohle River, outside Townsville, in North Queensland.

Like most Aboriginal people, the pressures on Nick to conform were huge. To get away from this pressure he had to find space somewhere. Nick could never really find that space and so he hanged himself. There, where he used to go down the beach all the time. The Bohle. He was twenty-eight.

Although I didn't see it right away, there was beauty in his death, too, because he hanged himself on land down the beach by the mouth of the river where we had all the good times.

That land was owned by two white people. We called them our Uncle Arthur and Aunty Joyce. The fact that they were white never entered our minds. We loved and cared for each other and that's what counted. They gave us free run of the place. We ran for miles up and down that beach. And there was beautiful rainforest there and bushland and mangroves. The smell was so sweet.

Uncle Arthur and Aunty Joyce leased this land; I think it was the meatworks that owned it. This land had been in their family for years. Uncle Arthur's father had leased it before him. They had a gate with a padlock on it to stop people coming through their land, but Uncle Arthur always let us know where the key was. It felt like we belonged there. They had fish traps that stretched from the mangroves out to the sea and whenever we arrived to set up camp, they made sure they'd left us a big barramundi or turtle or dugong.

When Uncle Arthur died, the developers, 'the unseen people' as Mum calls them, took over all that area. The leases were stopped and it was sold off.

Nicky couldn't handle that happening to our special place. He put that in his suicide note. He hated all our land being sold off to the Japanese. It's not their fault that they buy it. It's the fault of the Australian government wanting to sell our land off overseas in the first place.

Then in 1988, the Bicentennial year, my brother Paul, who fought really hard to make things right, hanged himself. He was also twenty-eight. Budda Paul, we used to call him. Budda is our way of saying 'brother'. Budda did everything that the white society asked of him. And they still never left him alone. He was one of the best actors, black or white, a great dancer and didjeridoo player and a brilliant storyteller. He had so many strings to his bow. He had the ability to cross all boundaries in expressing Aboriginal culture. But the pressure became too much for him.

In the back of his mind, somehow, he always knew that he too would have to endure the atrocities that happened to our people in the past. A long time ago, those atrocities were more out in the open. Now, in Paul's time, mind-games are used to trick and subdue Aboriginal people. A lot of the white people he worked with in the film industry never knew of the harassment he had to face, being black. It became too much for him. And he hanged himself.

My sister Kim was thirty-eight when she suicided in 1994. We called her Mimby. She was a brilliant artist and her spirit was so giving that her beauty shone beyond her laughter. With her art she was trying to create a business, which is hard being a woman. Being an Aboriginal woman, it's even harder. Kimmy had lots of plans and ideas for the future for her and her son, Nicky Bidju. It's

3

hard to pinpoint one thing that caused her to hurt herself, because so many dark shadows were cast over her. As time went on, the shadows became heavier. She had no space to breathe any fresh air into her body. Kimmy hanged herself under our parents' house.

Then came the loss of my nephew Liam in 1996. He was only thirteen. The police were chasing the stolen car he and two other boys were in. The boys' car crashed into a tree. Liam was the oldest of three brothers. The other two, Kurtis and Sean, were only nine and ten. Chicky, their mum, used to call the three of them Huey, Louie and Dewey because they were inseparable and in times of trouble they stuck together like glue. Chicky is on her own with the boys and so Liam, being the oldest, was like the protector of the family.

When I speak about the deaths of these four special people who died in four very bad ways before their time, it's not to make people say, 'Oh, poor little blackfulla' or to make us look like victims. What I want people to do is to really sit down and ask, 'Why did these people die?' Because it is an important part and structure of this country. I'm not just speaking about my family. Most Aboriginal families I know have lost one or two people in the same way. As an Aboriginal family you expect that. You really do expect that.

These four people had so much to give. Not only as Aboriginal people but as human beings. That's a point to remember. They were Aboriginal, but above and beyond that they were human beings. These four people had lots of good stories and secrets of this land. It's not just the death of a human being, it's the death of all that dies with them. It takes a lot out of me when I speak of these things. I had to watch my brother die – my younger brother Paul – and Nick as well. And I had a feeling that my sister would die, too. The death of my nephew Liam came straight out of nowhere. Him dying so young tears at my heart.

I get my strength to stay focused from my mum and dad and from my beautiful godson, Ciaran. And from the kids I perform for at all the schools. Also from the teachers. It's important to honour the teachers who work so hard and get no accolades. They probably don't want accolades anyway. All they want is to see things getting better in this country.

I think the most important thing is for Aboriginal people and non-Aboriginal people to realise that it is a simple thing to do, to make things better. Stop and think about it. You can't change the whole picture all at once. It's like getting a bucket of ice-cream and saying, 'Open your mouth. Here eat this.' The whole bucket is too much in one mouthful. What you've got to do is offer a spoonful at a time and gently feed it to people in quantities they can digest.

Start with the basics. Look at the Aboriginal history from your own area and then you can go on and flow out into the bigger picture, which is the rest of Australia. There's a bigger picture than Australia, too. There's the rest of the world which we're connected to now. Going beyond Australia to the rest of the world, that's huge. But to have your strength, you've got to start from your own area.

If people can see the beauty of Aboriginal culture, which is this country, then this will be a much happier place. The land and Aboriginal culture go hand in hand. You can't separate them. The land is the giver of life. It is our mother. It's like the vein of life. If you cut this, if you separate these two things, we die.

That's what this book is about.

When we were young fullas in our twenties, my brother Paul used to always push me and say, 'Come on', and he'd show me our dances. He was younger than me. But my idea then was to make my way in the mainstream of white society. I became a DJ while he went on performing – dancing, storytelling and didj playing in the schools. Anyway, after he died, I found myself taking up what he'd been doing, this schools' program, with my cousin Joe Geia. I stepped in and we started doing it as a duo. Eventually, I ended up performing by myself and continuing a lot of what my brother and cousin had put together, but restructuring the program to suit my abilities.

I liken my situation to track-and-field. Everybody is in a lane that they concentrate on. My older sisters are in lanes to do with politics, and my mum and dad as well. As respected elders, my parents are also spokespeople for all aspects of our culture. When my brother Paul died, he left his lane empty. I was in a lane in the city doing really well DJing and surviving on the white side of things. When he died, I had to pick up the baton and cross lanes because that work of performing in the schools is really important. It was good for me to do that. I went back home and learnt a lot of the things I'd missed by going away. I think that's a reason, too, that Paul left. Not so much that he knew, but I can hear him saying, 'Eh, you fulla, take this on.' I wasn't as talented as he was in dancing and acting, but the years of working in nightclubs gave me skills at reading audiences and their moods, as well as using my voice. I knew that to help make this a better place I had to continue on where Paul had left off.

It's very simple. The basic message I base my performances around is this: To feel happy about yourself, you must feel happy about the place you live in. To feel happy about the place you live in, you must get to know that place. To get to know that place, you must ask the people who have lived there the longest, the Aboriginal people. We have the key that can open the door to the treasures of this land.

2

WHERE I START

My main asset in the role I play as storyteller,
is that I'm not angry.

The other day this little one asked me, 'When did you start being an Aborigine and how old were you when you started that?' Like it was a career path or something. I just cracked up laughing.

Your blackness is always there. Nothing has to be said. You don't just wake up one morning and say, 'Hey, I'm an Aborigine!' In our family, you always knew you were different, but you knew we were strong. Even when I was a young boy, I knew that I was Kunggandji on my mother's side, from Yarrabah, and Birri-gubba on my dad's side, from the Bowen area.

We're a pretty big family, seven girls – can you believe I have seven sisters? – and only four of us boys. The relations from both my mother's and father's sides together form a pretty big mob of people. Questions are always

9

asked of me about relationships within family groups. White people try to put the groupings in boxes, like cousins, second cousins, third cousins and so on. But to us, a cousin is a cousin, an uncle is an uncle and an aunty is an aunty. We know we all belong to each other and that is our strength, you see. Because of this big mob that we are part of, the impact of attitudes when I was growing up was lessened because we had each other and we knew where we came from.

Listening to the old people is the true way of respect. That's the main message I like to get across when I speak about my culture. I say, 'There's three things that you have to remember. Three things that you have to do in life: Respect your elders. Respect each other. And respect the things that are living around you. If you don't do those three things then you're stuffed.' People laugh at the way I say, 'you're stuffed', but they get the message.

You have to live with each other. You have to learn off your elders and you have to live off the things around you. If you make the points short and sweet they stick in people's minds.

I tell the kids, if you don't listen, then you're never going to learn. Like, for example, in their class, if there is a kid playing up, the teacher might say to that child, 'Okay, you go over and stand in the corner and see me after school. Then go out and pick up papers in the yard and after that you can go home.' Or something along those lines. But if you are in the bush and you don't listen, then you die. There's no picking up papers, there's

10

no, 'Go stand in the corner'. If you eat the wrong berries, then you die, and if you don't know how to hunt the right way, then you die. If you don't listen, you die.

Aboriginal culture was intense, it was very strict and it was very strong. To survive this long it had to be strong. There was a lot of love as well but that strictness was there and it still is now.

Children in Aboriginal culture don't have a say, as such, but they have a role to play, as does everyone within the group. By having this role to play they do actually have a say within the circle of life. Being part of the group is all important. If one falters then everyone suffers. That's what you are taught as a kid. My dad used to say to me, 'You've got the rest of your life to be a grown-up. Now's the time for you to be a child.'

Even though in some cases we got a clip behind the ear or a whack on the bum with a stick for not listening, the important messages always got through to us. I can never remember any of us kids getting bitten by a snake or standing on a stone fish or getting stung really badly. That's pretty incredible when you think we lived in the tropics where there are many things that can harm you. But we were taught where to go and what to look out for.

There is a fine line between enthusiasm and respect. Having no respect can get you into trouble or even cost you your life. Enthusiasm without respect, just rushing into a situation head-on, can be equally as dangerous. Once, enthusiasm nearly cost me my life.

11

We were down the Bohle at Uncle Arthur and Aunty Joyce's. They had fish traps set and they told us we could help ourselves to whatever was there. The traps consisted of tree stakes stuck into the sand. There would be a row of them going way out across the water. There were three enclosures each about two metres square with chicken wire covering them. Once the fish swam into the trap, they couldn't get out because of the way the wire was facing into the enclosure.

When we arrived we would always go and check the fish traps first off. I could never wait to see what was caught. This time, I ran out ahead of the others. The water was up to my knees but I knew the tide was going out and that within minutes the water would be round my ankles. It was still early morning and quite dark. I pushed my way into the trap through the chicken wire and waited for my dad, who had the hurricane lamp, so that I could see what was caught in the trap.

Suddenly I heard my dad calling me, urgently. 'Stop there. Don't move. Come back slowly. Don't take your eyes off that one there.' I looked, and sure enough there were two eyes poking up from the water on the other side of the fish trap. It was a crocodile. My eyes never left it as I pushed myself back through the wire. That wire scratched me and it hurt, but I suppose it would have been more painful to lose a leg or an arm or maybe everything. Eventually, Uncle Arthur went back to get his rifle, then he came back and shot the crocodile and we all had a good feed. For years later, the head of the crocodile sat on a tree stump down there. Over the years the skull turned all white. Every time I walked past, I patted its head and thought, 'Unlucky you. Lucky me.'

You see, as a young fulla you learn not to go in front. Always walk behind your dad or your elders in the bush. You don't do anything unless your elders tell you. If you do something that you're not supposed to, it could be trouble not only for you but for someone else as well.

I see those ads on television and in tourist brochures, 'Where the rainforest meets the sea'. They have these romantic images with people lying out on the beach, relaxing. I have a good laugh to myself. They never show you the stingers, the sharks or the crocs. On dusk, the mosquitoes that come out are big enough to carry you away, not to mention the sandflies which attack in great numbers and eat you alive. We used to put cow manure on the fire and that smoke would keep the mozzies away. The old people used the bases of different trees that give off powerful smoke when they burn. That smoke keeps everything away.

I remember those nights by the fire when we would curl up with our bellies full and listen while the adults told us stories. They were the best times. Having lots of aunties and uncles meant that there were a lot of tricks played on us younger ones. Lots of scary stories about Quinkins with red eyes, which was really my Uncle Neil walking towards us, smoking a cigarette. They would say he was the one-eyed Quinkin and all us kids would believe them. Sometimes we'd be in the tent with Mum telling us stories and, I suppose like all children, we loved the scary ones. Right on cue, my uncle would scratch the tent and make groaning noises.

They say our people traditionally told scary stories to their children to keep them close to the camp and not go wandering off where they could get hurt or lost. By the time this tradition got to our family, our uncle in particular seemed to think it was just for a good laugh, I reckon. At the same time, there were spirits that really did come to our house, some bad spirits, some good spirits, and we were very aware of these as young children. These stories by the fire served a very important purpose in my life.

I know I draw on these experiences I had as a child when I perform now. When I'm performing I can feel the power of my family there with me. It's not just me standing up there telling stories. It's all of us.

The way we look at it is that everyone is part of a circle and everyone is important to that circle no matter what you do. My strength is that I am a storyteller, a communicator. I can play the didjeridoo and sing and dance, but my purpose is to be a storyteller.

When you start whispering and you can hear yourself and you can't hear anything else, that's when you know you've got your audience. You're not just telling a story. It's an amazing feeling. Sometimes you get lost within the story, too. You float along. You know the story when you're telling it but you float along. The story takes you over. It's funny, when you see this, you don't really see it but you feel it. They will open up their hearts and their minds and you go in there and that's a really nice place to be. You can do all these wonderful things in there, you know. You can really and truly play up and be stupid.

A couple of years ago, I was playing basketball and I twisted my ankle. When I performed I had to strap it up in a figure-of-eight bandage. I was doing this performance and in the middle of it this little boy had his hand up for a long time and so eventually I said, 'Yes, yes?' He asked, 'What happened to your foot?' I said, 'You don't really want to know what –' And the whole class goes, 'Yes, yes.' I said, 'Do you really want to know what happened?' And everybody started yelling out, 'Yes!' I was building them all up. 'You don't really want to know!' 'Yeeesss!!' So I said, 'Oh, well, okay then.'

I put down my sticks and I told them. 'Well. One day I was out hunting and I thought, look, I might try and get some goanna today for a feed. So I was tracking this goanna and, of course, you gotta be real careful, you know. There might be poisonous snakes around or other things that could hurt you. And I didn't know this particular day that there was a big, fat crocodile looking for this goanna, too. I was down near, not really near the mangroves, but near the salt water.

'Anyway I was sort of tracking him, the goanna, and thinking where he was going and how far away he was going and I had a feeling that there was somethin' else around. Something really scary.'

'Course as I was telling this story, I got down like the

15

crocodile and I'm doing the motions of the crocodile and then I do the goanna. I was making it up as I was going along. I had two hundred kids shut up and watching, and you could hear a pin drop. I was down to whispering and you could feel them going, "Cos here's this real man that was, like, with a real crocodile.' Anyway, I went on with the story.

'Finally, I threw the spear and of course I missed the goanna 'cos he was really fast. The goanna didn't know the crocodile was after him either. The goanna sort of turned around and came back the other way. And then I had a boomerang there so I tried to throw that at him, see. But the goanna ducked and I missed him with the boomerang, too.'

I made up this story about the goanna dodging these spears and so on, you know, 'wooow woow wooow wooow', doing kung-fu or something. And, of course, the kids loved it.

'Anyway, the crocodile got angry at me 'cos I was trying to take his food, so he attacked me and I kicked him in the snout. I don't know how, but I ended up falling off this cliff and landed on my leg and that's when I twisted my ankle. I was really in pain so I got some bush medicine and I rubbed it into my foot and wrapped it up in bark and . . .'

A bigger load of bull you never heard. So, anyway, after I finished, there was a deathly silence. Then a lot of kids went, 'woooooooo!', and I said, 'Well, now I've got it strapped up and I swim and try to keep it strong through exercise.' All the kids were looking at the bandage. It was like they were looking at me and breathing in and going, 'Wow, thank you for being so tough and so brave!'

At the end of the performance I said, 'Okay, children. There's one thing I've got to say to you. You know that story I was telling you about the crocodile?' They said, 'Yes.' 'Well, it wasn't true.' They said, 'What?' 'Well, I didn't do it like that. I actually did it playing basketball.' You could hear the groans going, 'oorrrrr'. So I said, 'But it was going one on one against Andrew Gaze.' And they said, 'It doesn't matter.' I'm sorry, Andrew, this time you were outdone by the crocodile, but that story took a lot of pain away from my ankle.

It was something spontaneous, something you don't plan. I was laughing with them. When you've got them and you're whispering and you're taken up by the story as well, it's like you've got a lump of clay in your hands that you can mould and knead and shape so it fits the story. You've got a hundred and fifty, a hundred and sixty, kids in this clay who are quite happy to be moulded and shaped like that. They love it.

Your telling of the story is caressing their inner self, their hearts and their souls and tickling them and laughing. Without specifically looking at any one child, you can see so much in all their faces. Sometimes you come out of the haze of telling a story and you look to see if they're still with you. 'Yep, they're still there.' Then you go back into this haze again. When I'm telling a really good story I'm fully, totally, absorbed in it.

17

My main asset in the role I play as storyteller is that I'm not angry. Well, of course I am angry at what happened to my people and what continues to happen today, but I turn that anger into a positive thing to give me the energy to communicate with people about our culture.

It's not who I am, it's what I'm talking about that is the most important thing. This culture, these stories, are from this land. It's not Ninja Turtle, it's not Bart Simpson, Mickey Mouse or Donald Duck. It's from the land we are on. To hear stories from and about your own country gives you a strong sense of belonging.

One mother came up to me with tears in her eyes. It was at the end of four days of storytelling, dancing, singing and painting that I had spent in this school. She gave me a big hug and said, 'Thank you for making my daughter feel like she belongs in this country. Every day my daughter comes home telling me stories word for word. "Mum, listen to this. Isn't this one great. These stories are from our land."'

This country can be in the hearts of everyone who lives here, not just a map stuck up on the wall. Most Australians have never been given anything that tells them they belong here. So little has been taught to them about this place.

Aboriginal people happen to be the first people here and have lived in this country for so many thousands of years – is it fifty thousand or sixty thousand years or longer? That's a long time to get to know a place. So, we have the secrets, the stories and all the knowledge you need to love this land, you see.

There are some sacred stories and dances that cannot be given and will be kept secret. But there's a lot that can be shared. Aboriginal people are very giving and sharing people. In the light of what has happened in the past, this is quite remarkable.

As a child I always knew where I belonged. You grow into an awareness of being Aboriginal, you grow into knowing about your culture from being around your mum and dad and your aunties and uncles. You know you are different because of the way kids treat you at school. And it doesn't take long for the police – we call them the bullymen or goolaji – to start picking you out. But I didn't get it so bad because my dad had established himself as a respected person in Townsville.

Dad was a hard worker and a tough fighter. He was a very talented boxer when he was a young man. I can remember seeing Dad spar in the ring when I was a little one. He was so quick on his feet that no one could touch him. He fought many of the great Aboriginal boxers, like Jack Hassan. He and Jack are still mates. They were both from Palm Island and had the same trainer.

I got a ride the other night in a taxi in Melbourne. The driver was an old pug, a prize fighter. We started talking about boxing. He remembered my dad as a young boxer. He said he could have gone on to be a great fighter. At the time he had to make a choice, doing the boxing circuit or being at home with Mum. In fact, my mother

19

remembers that they were about to get married and there was a big boxing carnival on. Mum told him to go to the carnival because she knew how important it was to him. But Dad decided to stay with her and get married. Mum says:

> He's never once said to me, 'If it wasn't for you, I could have been a great boxer.' He's only ever said, 'I loved you and that's the choice I wanted to make and it was a good one.' We had a little tiny wedding. We never had much money. His trainer paid for the taxi for us to get to the church. What a lovely man.

Dad worked on construction sites as a jack-of-all-trades when I was young. He was a person of position not only around the town but also within our own black community. The Garbutt mob we called ourselves, after Garbutt, the suburb of Townsville where all the black-fullas and some poor whites lived. Dad could work and drink and fight with the best of them. So, sometimes it was easier for me because I was Monty Pryor's son.

Later on my dad became a deacon in the Catholic church. He tells how it came about like this:

> I was working for a construction mob. This young Catholic priest, Father Mick Peters, was looking for Catholic Aboriginals. I'd been brought up Catholic. He came along to my work, so I asked the boss if

I could have an hour off to sit and talk to the priest. I'd always been a hard worker, so the boss said yes. Me and the priest sat and yarned. The young priest wanted me to work for the church visiting the hospital and the prison, and to help with services. I told him to give me a couple of weeks to think about it.

I'd been an altar boy as a kid so I knew about the church. The main thing I wanted to do was to give some respect back to my church. I talked about it with the family. They thought it was a good idea. So, I finished up with the construction job and started work with the church. I was about sixty then.

The bishop had a chat with me after a while. He said, 'We want people like you who have the experience and know how to speak to the people. You respect people and they respect you.' This was after about four years of working with the church. You see, he wanted me to become a deacon. When I decided to take it on, it was because I believed we are all one people. Everyone is a human being. We've got to try and help each other.

This is funny, though. I remember when I was a young bloke, I was working out on a cattle station. There was an elder there who was in the church. He asked me when I was going to go to church. I said, 'Blow that! God don't pay my

21

wages.' So, years later when I was back over home and I'd become a deacon, I came across this same elder. He said, 'He's not a bad bloke to work for is he?' We had a good laugh together.

My dad told me since I was a little kid, 'You've got to work harder and be tougher than them', than the white people. And I learnt that, too. So I've always had that approach. Even when I was cleaning floors, I'd clean them better than anyone else that was cleaning floors. I still try to have that drive. I know it's there with me when I'm performing.

I've had the opportunity to perform for all ages in most states of Australia over the past six years. You'd be amazed at what a lot of people in this country don't know about our history. When I say history, I mean black as well as white history. There are a lot of people, black and white, who are trying to correct this imbalance of knowledge. Two people working very hard in the field of education are Diedre Mahon and Alesha Warburton. They work within Catholic Education training other primary school teachers to seek the right approach in teaching Aboriginal Studies.

Diedre told me about these surveys she does with primary school children. Two weeks before a training session with the teachers, she surveys their children asking them questions like, 'What do you know about Aboriginal people?' No names, no classes, just their responses. The responses are quite terrifying. Some of them are things like, 'all Aboriginal people eat humans', 'they live in Africa'. 'They're all dead' is quite common. 'There's no real ones left', 'they eat their babies'. You have to ask yourself why the answers to these questions are so horrific and totally incorrect. This is 1996 we're talking about.

White people often think that we are all the same. But not all Aboriginal people dance the same and not all Aboriginal people speak the same language or sing the same songs. Not all Aboriginal people play the didjeridoo. Not all Aboriginal people paint the same. Though we are all Aboriginal people, our cultures are different. The common thread that unites us all across the country is our respect for the land and the living things around us that we depend on to survive.

Australia is an enormous place with over six or seven hundred different Aboriginal groups. You don't really know until you start travelling across the country. Isn't it huge? Each group has its own area and before two hundred years ago, if you were to cross somebody's land without permission there would be war. There was special protocol to observe as a visitor. The lighting of fire was a common custom to alert the people whose land you were going to walk on. There would be a sit-down to discuss your purpose in crossing their land and to exchange gifts before the right of passage was given.

Visitors were told where they could go on the land they were crossing and where to stay away from.

Still today, it's important to acknowledge whose land you are on, wherever you are. For example, when I perform in Melbourne, I take care to acknowledge that I am on Wurundjeri land, not only through the community of Aboriginal people but also by explaining it to whoever I'm performing in front of.

Every part of the culture – the songs, dances, the way of painting – is particular to the group and the place they come from. One example of this is the unique sound of the didjeridoo. My mother's group, the Kunggandji people, traditionally use this instrument and it is called the yikki yikki. But my dad's group, the Birri-gubba, don't use it and neither do many groups across this land.

Each group has many different dances. There are dances for fun, ceremonial dances, burial dances, thanking-spirits-for-food dances, welcoming, farewelling, calling the spirits in, putting them back . . . Some of the ceremonial dances can only be danced on certain occasions.

Our group, the Kunggandji people, have a dance called the Katcha, which means the spirit or the ghost dance. When we do this dance we ask all the spirits who are in the earth to come up and sit down while we perform. We do this to ask permission to dance on the land. If we didn't do this it would be like jumping all over the spirits of our ancestors and something bad might happen. After we have finished our dancing we pick the spirits up and throw them back. Once we say that last word of that song, we can't do no more dancing until we do that dance again, that Katcha Dance.

A spirit dance is about any kind of animal that is living – snake, crocodile, goanna – any living thing. You're dancing its spirit. We do that because it is the animals that teach us how to hunt. By watching and listening we are taught their ways. Then by mimicking the kangaroo through dance – smelling like the kangaroo and carrying the spear hidden under your foot as you hop – you are able to approach the animal without it noticing you. Then you can spear the animal. In some groups, different animals carry different messages or warnings, so we are connected in that spiritual way also.

Story dances tell stories. This is how we communicate without talking to each other, through body language, even though we don't understand each other's languages. A story dance is telling the story of what actually happened on a day, like writing it out; you actually write out what happened on that day.

The Honey Dance I do is a good dance because it shows how our songs and dances keep evolving even through the arrival of other people to this land. The native bee is a tiny little black bee that doesn't have a sting. When the black and yellow bee arrived with the Europeans, we had to find a new way of gathering honey. A story dance was made up to warn other groups about this new bee with the sting, which makes this story dance only about a hundred and eighty years old.

When you're watching a dance it's like a library book.

You're sitting down and you're reading it like a book. The pages, the chapters, the verses – they're all in there. All you've got to do is to work out how to read it. You read it through expressions of movement, song and dance. That cuts out the language barrier. And sometimes with the dance, there might be a painting to go with it. Within that painting there might be a dance to go with it as well as the story, a song and characters. Not all the time, though. Sometimes the painting tells a story without any dancing or singing.

Stories, dances and paintings teach you about the foods you can and can't eat, as well. You could die by eating the wrong berry or going into the wrong places. The food you eat depends on where you are. That applies wherever you are, even in the city, as I found out one day in the playground of this primary school.

I was out getting some leaves for the dancing. These kids come belting across the playground to see what I'm doing. The first little fulla came up and said, 'Hello, Mont.' I said, 'How you going, mate?' He said, 'Good.' Just behind him was this little girl. She yelled out, 'What's Monty doing?' The other little fulla behind her answered her question in a very protective voice, 'Leave him. He's getting something to eat.' I had a laugh to myself and said, 'You fullas go back inside now', and off they went. At lunchtime, I went up to the milk bar to get something to eat. There was a mum there who was coming in to school to help. Later, she was back in the class and she said to the kids, 'Guess who I saw up the milk bar getting something to eat?' They said, 'Who?' She said, 'Monty. He was getting a hamburger.' This little one said, 'But he already had something to eat.' I said to the mum, she should have told him the koalas ate all the good food, so I was still hungry!

It's not just these little ones that get confused. I have adults coming up to me asking the same sort of questions about what I eat. What you eat depends on where you are. Our group was on the coast – we are saltwater people and had plenty of food to choose from. The mangroves, my favourite spot, was a supermarket. Then you had the saltwater river, then the reef, the freshwater creek and not forgetting the bush tucker. So you can see it was plentiful. In the middle, in the desert, they have to be very careful about their food and water. If I went on to their land, they would teach me what to hunt and where to hunt. The bush medicine would be different also.

The turtle and dugong were two of our many food sources. When I tell the children about hunting the turtle they go, 'Yuck. You killed turtles.' They all screw their faces up and I just say, 'Okay, all of you kids that eat meat put your hand up.' Almost all of them put their hands up. And I say, 'Put your hand up if you go out and kill your own food. If you go out and grab the sheep, cut its throat and bleed it.' And they all go, 'ooooo'. And I say, 'Look, somebody's got to kill that sheep for you. I know when you go shopping with your parents and you go to the butcher shop then your parents might say, "Can I have a kilo of this and a leg of this and a whatsisname of that?"'

It's when you actually have to kill something that you respect that creature. When you have to hold something down while it's struggling to get away and you kill it. That's when you learn respect. That creature gives up its life for you to live. I worked in an abattoir when I was young. Let me tell you, it's not a pretty sight. If any of you were to go into an abattoir and see what has to be done, then the next day you'd all be eating leaves and trees.

I remember Dad taught me about this with a turtle, and its name wasn't Donatello or Michelangelo. I was about six or seven. I had to smash its head and cut its throat. You imagine that turtle on its back gulping blood and squirming, and it's not a very good sight. He said, 'Come here, boy. You got to learn how to do this. This is what you got to learn.'

And I learned how to cut him up and how to take out this and that. After a while you respected that turtle because he gave up his life for you. That's what a lot of kids don't realise now. People on the farms, they see a lot of births and deaths and killing things. It becomes a bit more sanitised in the big city. That's where the disrespect for life comes. Not the respect for it. The disrespect for it. It comes from being sanitised.

That reverence for life and death is still with us as Aboriginal people. That continues through the rest of your life, too. Respecting your elders, respecting other people, respecting other people's things. It was drummed into you from a very young age, that respect.

Of course, times have changed, but the messages still

stay the same and are as important now as they were back then. The givers of life are the most important, for without them there can be no life.

My nephew Sean was fishing with his mum. He caught this big fish. He pulled him up and was really excited saying, 'Mum, look, look, I've caught this big fish.' My sister looked at the fish and immediately put the fire of his enthusiasm out by saying, 'No. That's a girl fish. You gotta throw him back.' So, Sean, with a real slack look on his face, held the fish up, looked into its eyes and said, 'You lucky you not a man.' He kissed the fish and threw it back into the water.

It's hard for white people to see that we live in two worlds when they think our traditional lifestyle and culture is gone. They see us living in the white way and often they don't realise that we are still living by the beliefs and ways of our ancestors. Our bodies are living the way they want us to live but our hearts and souls still stay the old way. So you get all this talk about who is a real Aborigine and who isn't. You find yourself having to explain who you are and what you are to all kinds of people, young and old.

This little one, she was six years old. I'd finished a performance for her class and I had my clothes on ready to go home. As I was walking past I remembered her and said, 'Did you like the show?' 'Yes,' she said. Then I said,

'What part of the show did you like?' 'Everything.' And I said, 'Oh, that's nice.' Then she said, 'But you're not a real Aborigine, are you?' So I said, 'Yes, I am.' And she said, 'No, you're not.' I found myself having to defend my Aboriginality with this six-year-old. You remember the old saying, never go head to head with children or animals, you'll always lose.

She kept going, 'Before you were, but now you're not.' And I went, 'aaah'. So, I tried a different tack with this little one. I said, 'Well, when you go home and go to bed, do you put your pyjamas on?' And she said, 'Yes.' 'And when you come to school do you wear your uniform to school?' 'Yes.' And I said, 'Do you ever wear your school uniform to bed?' 'No!' 'Do you ever wear your pyjamas to school?' She said, 'No!!' Like really adamant, 'No!!!' 'Well,' I said, 'it's the same with Aboriginal people. When I perform for you I dress the way we dress when we do dances. Now I've finished showing you how we dance so I put these clothes on. This is how I usually look unless I'm doing dancing.'

I could see the penny drop and she went, 'oh', knowingly. She walked around me and then went off happily.

This other little red-headed fulla came up to me. I remembered him from the dancing. He was really good. He looks up at me after I've changed back into my tracksuit. 'But you're not a real Aborigine.' He answers his own question. 'Well, no you're not.' I can't get a word in. 'Well, how come you're driving a car?' He keeps on going. 'Well, I suppose it's easier than walking around.

Well, see ya.' And he walks off. I didn't have to say a thing. Aren't they funny, those little ones?

There was this little Aboriginal kid. His mum and I were talking after the show and I said, 'He's a lovely boy that one.' I remember him because he came up and did some dances really well. And she said, 'You know what that "lovely boy" said? And I slapped him across the ear for it, too. He come up and he said, "Mum, guess what? A real Aborigine's coming to school today." And I said to him, "What? You're a real Aborigine! Don't you worry about being real. You are real!"'

I think that concept has been pushed into the heads of Aboriginal kids. You're not a real Aborigine if you're not standing on a boulder, one leg up, leaning against a spear. You're not a real Aborigine unless you stamp your feet, throw spears and paint up.

I've had that before, that kind of comment. I took a mob of dancers from up home, from Kunggandji, down to this hostel in Geelong to perform. One of these young blokes from the hostel said, 'It's going to be great having some real Aborigines here.' And this was a hostel just for Aboriginal kids. But it's like, 'Oh, the real Aborigines are coming.' And I said, 'But you are one, too.' He wasn't convinced.

Those two little fullas, they're within every one of us blackfullas because that confusion of identity has been put there through one way or other. We're always told that you're not a real Aboriginal unless you're a full blood. And yet at the same time, not so long ago, being a full blood also meant that you were regarded as a savage and you had to be bred out or killed. But the only way you're accepted as an Aboriginal now is if you are a full blood! So what can you do? You're not black. You're not white. You're this thing in the middle with clothes on.

A friend of mine, Tommy Lewis, is from the Northern Territory, from the Roper River area. Walking around Melbourne no one would ever doubt he is a blackfulla. He has very black skin. But he says that because he was one of the first people in his group to have a white father, he was always called a whitefulla when he was growing up. It wasn't till he was about twelve and he went into Darwin to school that he got called a blackfulla. There were three other children in his group with white fathers but they were taken away from their families when they were very young. Tommy says he was lucky. The school teacher, who was a white woman, would tell his mother when the government people were coming around to take the children away. Then his mum would take him into the bush and camp out or hide him in a canoe and paddle down the river. He talks a lot about being between two cultures.

At one school a young white girl asked, 'Can a real Aboriginal be white?' Apparently she had seen an Aboriginal dance group and the performers were all different shades of colour. I answered her question by using an example of a young boy who was going to the very same school that she was. His name is Anton. His mother can identify her tribe and has kept in contact with all of her elders back in her country, her place. Anyway, someone in his class had asked that question, 'Can Aboriginal people be white?' So, he put up his hand and he said, 'Well, here I am.' And the kids said, 'What?' He's very fair. He's got blue eyes and freckles. The first time the teachers had talked to him about his Aboriginality, he didn't know the name of his tribe or his country. He would say, 'Oh, yes, Mum knows that.' The teachers commented that after my next visit, he'd found out a lot more for himself. I think me being there and talking about the strength I get from my place inspired him to look out for himself and his own heritage.

In Anton's case his mother knew her background and was happy to pass it on to him. All he had to do was ask. Sometimes the parents don't wish their children to identify as Aboriginal. I was down the south coast of Victoria performing at a school. I'd finished and was talking to the children as I usually love to do, when this little one burst forward. She must have been about seven or eight years old. She said out loud, 'I'm an Aborigine.' I knelt down and said, 'Hello, my sister. How are you?' As I did that I could hear all the other children go silent, then together say, 'Are you?' And she said yes, really proudly. After we had a little discussion she walked off with all of her friends gathered around her. Later I found out from a teacher that her parents had asked that she not be identified as Aboriginal. She must have thought in her mind that it was okay because all of her friends were very interested in Aboriginal culture. So she took it upon herself to embrace her Aboriginality.

I love performing at schools where there are lots of Aboriginal children. For me it's good to see them and for them it's good to see me. It's a dual thing. I sit down and talk to all the kids after all the shows I do, but for me it's really special when Aboriginal children are there.

I was at this beautiful school in Sydney near the Royal National Park. The teachers were just wonderful. After the performance the children were all coming up and wanting to talk. This little one said, 'Thank you, Monty.' She was about seven, I suppose. All the other kids were around. I looked at her and gave her a big hug. She looked up at me with her beautiful eyes and said, 'Can you make me an Aborigine?'

I looked down at her and I thought, 'This little one has something special.' It wasn't just a whim. She really felt that what she had seen was beautiful. So I knelt down and I gave her another hug and said, 'Look, really, I can't make you an Aborigine. But I think deep inside you're asking questions and you're listening and you're learning. It's sort of making you into an Aboriginal person in your heart. Because that's what everybody has to do, is be open. Then the learning will come.'

I felt wonderful about this. I went out to my car, Trusty Rusty, and got a T-shirt from the Laura Festival, an Aboriginal cultural festival which is held every two years in Laura, up near Cooktown, near my homeland. I gave the T-shirt to her and she squealed, 'Thank you!' As she was going back I saw her throw off her jumper and put the T-shirt on over the rest of her clothes.

The children give me a lot. I love how they explain what they see. Like this one day when a lot of these little ones were asking me why I had black skin. One of them noticed that the palms of my hands were white. This beautiful little one said, 'That's because when they came around to paint you, you were busy and they missed under your hands.'

What I give them from my culture brings out lots of expression through artwork and letters they send me. I sit down and look at every one. Every one is important to me. I appreciate that the children communicate back to me through their drawings and writings. That means that they listen. And it's what I mean about them open-ing up. I need *them* to heal for *me* to heal, you know what I mean? They are the light that shows me the way through that room of darkness.

We trust each other. If you let them look into your heart, they'll show you into theirs. They can see that I open up my heart and I say, 'You come in here.' And they come in. And then they open up their heart and I jump in there and that's a good place to be.

Sometimes I look into these children's eyes and I try to see myself. I think about what I was like at that point of time in my life. I feel like some of my childhood was taken away from me, personal things, things that shouldn't happen to young kids. I want to stop that from happening to these young ones.

Sometimes children come to me and I look into their eyes – it's the window to their heart – and I can see their hurt and they see the same in me. It seems like we exchange scars or exchange wounds because then we know we both have been to that same place. They know they are safe with me because I understand where they are.

You can't go back and rearrange what happened. All you can do is make it better and make amends for what happened. The way to do that is through listening to each other. That's where the openness comes in. If they see that you're open then they'll be open with you. They'll give you things. You don't come in with all this gear or anything. It's a blackfulla way of teaching – just a hollow stick, a bunch of leaves and me – with a good sense of humour.

To teach anything about Aboriginal people you have to know us and our culture. Everyone hears the kooka-burra but you've got to listen to the kookaburra if you want to teach anyone about it.

There is truth in the saying that the things that scare you the most are the things you don't know much about. This was with a group of kindergarten kids, kinders, to Grade 2s in a very culturally diverse school. At the end of the show, this little one, his name was Abdul, he jumped up and came running out. All the children were around me and he was trying to say something. So, I asked the others to move and I brought him in close and they made a circle around us. Then I knelt down and said, 'Yes, mate?' And he looked at me and said, 'You know . . . you know . . . um . . . um . . .' He was trying to get it out in a hurry as the teachers were organising the children to move back to their classes.

'You know what . . . um . . . um . . . before, you know, I used to be really scared of Aboriginal people. And . . . um . . . I remember . . . when I used to see Aborigines on TV I used to pull the sheet up and hide underneath and . . . um . . . I used to be really frightened.'

After all this, he just looked up into my face and said, 'But I'm not scared any more.'

I gave him a big hug. He just wanted to tell me. I thought it was great he wanted to come up and tell me: I'm not scared of you any more, I'm not scared of Aboriginal people any more.

3

WHERE I GO FROM THERE

*A lot of people have suffered and died for me to
be able to keep these songs and dances.*

It takes a lot to stand up there and face a hundred and
fifty, two hundred kids, just in my judda jah – my little
red undies – and nothing else on except this paint. When
I say paint, I mean this ochre that comes from the earth.
When I put it on, nothing can touch me. It's my shield or
my plate of armour. It's something no one can take from
me, my link to the strength from the past. Believe me,
you need it. You've never met any of these students
before in your life and you're standing up there in your
underpants. Sometimes you'll be standing up there in
front of a whole school of adolescent girls.

Adolescence is a strange time in every child's life. The
collecting of influences that direct you in future life is
important. In my teenage years I had two worlds to
gather these influences from. It was like one minute I

was out playing football or sitting up in a school uniform learning maths and science – not that I was crazy about either of those two subjects – and the next minute I was in the bush learning about hunting and how to cut up turtle or dugong.

My older cousin Mervyn used to look after me. I was the oldest boy in my family, so Mervyn became my big brother. I knew that if any troubles were too much for me, then I'd have him to back me up. But he got me a lot of floggings, too. Every time I see him now we sit down and have a talk and I remind him, 'Remember when you conned me into breaking into the tuckshop? And remember when we stripped the wiring out of that new place they were building and melted the copper and sold it at Churchies?' Of course I never said no, but it feels good shifting the blame onto my older cousin. He always denies it at first and then eventually goes, 'Oh yeah . . .'

My adolescent years were confusing times on another level. Back then, Aboriginal people weren't regarded as Australians. The struggle for my people even to be regarded as human beings was intense, let alone having the right to vote. There were many lives lost leading up to this point in time when, in 1967, a National Referendum was held, and finally Aboriginal people were recognised as Australian citizens with the right to vote.

I didn't know what it all meant at the time. But I knew something big was happening and we were all fighting for something. I knew you had to look after yourself because of the police authority within Townsville and on the reserves as well, Yarrabah and Palm Island.

I remember growing up as a time of confusion. You were there but you weren't really there. My people had been on this land for at least fifty to sixty thousand years and yet white people, who had only been here two hundred years, were telling us we didn't exist until they had a majority vote to say we were Australians. I don't know about you, but to me that is confusing!

We grew up as a really good family, although we had our problems. Having a strong family unit as well as extended family, we drew strength from each other in the difficult times. We still went out bush nearly every weekend. We'd go up to Yarrabah if we had a car, and over to Palm Island. We'd go down to the Bohle – you know, Uncle Arthur and Aunty Joyce's place at the mouth of the river near Townsville – if we couldn't get back up to Yarrie or Palm. We'd pick Burdekin plums, Chonkie apples, go fishing, trapping, or down to the mangroves. It was special. My mum and dad were not living in the bush traditionally but they know a lot. And because my uncles and aunties still live in Yarrabah and have never left there, they know a lot more.

My mother tells me stories about my great-grandmother Jinnah Katchwan. She was the first Kunggandji woman to be brought down from the hills onto the mission at Yarrabah. On Yarrabah, in those days, like many other reserves, we weren't allowed to do our dances, sing our songs, do any ceremonies or speak our language. If you got caught doing any of these, you were punished severely. Women having their heads shaved and wearing a sugar bag for a dress was a common punishment. The men would be imprisoned on a diet of bread and water for the crime of keeping their culture.

This thing of deprivation of your culture is deeply embedded, you know. I was confused for a long time myself. That confusion reigns supreme within your mind. It just doesn't let you have faith in yourself.

I was one of the first Aboriginal students to go to Pimlico High School in Townsville. The transition from primary school to high school was made easier for me because I played football with a lot of the boys in the local clubs. Because I was good at sport, that let me have some faith in myself and helped me deal with my situation.

Most of the kids that came to school, their dads worked with my dad. He worked on construction sites and he knew everybody in town, so that helped, too. The first few months were a bit tough. I had to stand up for myself. That meant a few knuckle-ups. Some I lost, some I drew and some I won. But it was okay after that because you play footy and you play basketball and you prove yourself that way. Football was a way of having equality in the community.

I played Aussie Rules for Garbutt, a suburb of Townsville, which was also the name for the Aboriginal football team. I think it showed me a way of staying out of trouble, that's what I liked about it. With sport you have to play on the weekends, especially because I ended up playing both sports – football and basketball. Even though it meant I couldn't go bush as much, I loved it. I had to be in shape so I couldn't go out and get charged up, get drunk. Of course, some people would play charged up, but that didn't work out so good sometimes.

Footy gave you that concept of playing with a team, too. It gave me an understanding of my skills and how to use them. If you had skills that were really good and perhaps better than a lot of other players, you still had to train and not cut corners, because you were part of a team. This I had to learn the hard way. I never liked doing warm-up exercises, tiger walks and push-ups. At the start of each training session, I used to hide behind a gum tree on the edge of the field and wait for these ful-las to move on to the real stuff of kicking the footy and playing games. One day, I got caught by the coach. From then on I had to do double the warm-up exercises that everyone else did. Strangely enough, my game improved immensely!

I played with and against non-Aboriginal people. The McDonald boys, Butchy and Jimmy, played a big role within the football team. Their mother, Mrs Mac, used to tie my bootlaces for me because I was always late for the games. There were some brilliant Aboriginal football players that played for Garbutt and could have played in any league in Australia. The Butler boys were the fastest runners. In my eyes, Ricco Butler was the best. He was a magician. Wally Tallis and Steve Lampton were also great players.

It got a bit rough because Garbutt used to have punch-ups sometimes, well, a lot of times, okay, heaps of times. You'd get slung off at because you were the Aboriginal team. That's where you learned to concentrate on not taking any abuse from anyone. Sport is an area in which Aboriginal people excel. So, to put you off your game you'd get called names, like 'abo', 'boong', 'darkie', 'chocolate', 'liquorice stick', and so on. This would make you lose your concentration – funny about that. What you had to do was think, well, the reason why this person is saying these things and calling you names is that the person marking you knows that you are going to beat them on the day. You learnt how to concentrate because if you didn't you'd react and start a fight and lose possession of the ball.

Our coach, he was a Murri fulla – when we say 'Murri' we mean one of us fullas from North Queensland – he used to tell us not to worry about being called names. 'They are giving you a compliment. That means you are beating them.' He'd tell us, 'Wait till the game is finished, then you can clean 'im up.' Sometimes, it was hard to wait till the end of the game!

I used to imagine them bashing me over the head with a big stick with every single word of abuse they could think of written on it. By not reacting and concentrating on my game and just playing football, I'd take

44

their stick away, I'd disarm them, I'd take their weapon off them. Then they were the ones who became weak.

When I was younger, sport was good, it gave me discipline, although I had discipline at home. You got to travel to other places and the picture of another world began to emerge in your mind. If you were going to be employed, sport gave you a way of being accepted. We had basketball carnivals in Ayr, Rockhampton and Mackay, all towns south of Townsville, also in the north, in Cairns. I went down to Brisbane to play in the State Championships for the Under 18s basketball team. Travelling to these places, especially Brisbane, expanded my horizons and to top it all off, it was great fun to be able to play sport and make friends.

I made a lifetime friend, Danny Underwood, playing football as a teenager. This was when I was playing for the Currajong football team. I had switched from Garbutt and played three or four years with Currajong before I left Townsville for the Air Force. Danny's family are whitefullas and were staunch supporters of right-wing politics. Even as teenagers we understood why our families were politically so different, and we respected that difference. We'd leave all that aside and go out and kick the footy.

Our friendship has lasted through many changes of government. When we see each other now, we still play the same way. He gives me a lecture about money and how even though I help my family when they are in need, I should look out for myself. I love him for caring for me, and then we laugh ourselves stupid over silly jokes, just like we did as teenagers.

At Pimlico High, the teachers were great – with a couple of exceptions. One in particular caused me a few problems. In sheet-metalwork one day, we were all lining up. He was yelling, 'Get in line.' One of my mates pushed me out of line. The teacher grabbed me and said, 'You trying to be smart?' He belted me one and threw me against the wall and knocked the wind out of me. He thought that was the end of it but my father had other ideas. By the time I got home that day, my dad knew about it and decided to balance the scales of justice. So he rode into school next morning and gave it to the teacher. When he left the sheet-metal room, after the smoke had cleared, the scales were balanced. All my mates yelled out, 'Wooow! Wish I had a dad like that. Can I borrow him?'

There was an English teacher who was very special – he was a wonderful man. He taught me how to use words instead of fists and he also had faith in me that I could write. I suppose through my eyes, at that time in my life, he was pretty uncool. He wore shorts and long white socks. I can't remember him ever laughing. All my mates thought he was really square – the way he spoke, his mannerisms and expressions – trying to teach this rabble the importance of using words. I never imagined back then that one day I would be standing up in schools in front of mobs of hormonally disturbed adolescents. At least he had his clothes on!

What I unknowingly learnt from teachers like this in high school were the tools to survive in the white world. What I learnt from my family were the tools to survive in the black world. How I make my living now is by using the tools that I was given from both worlds to shape my inner self and then to communicate this to other people.

What I have had to watch is that the white culture does not swamp my black heart. I've seen that happen to many of my people. That has meant not losing respect for either world. If you take one for granted, it will hurt you and the other one will forget you. I am very conscious of spending time in both worlds, respecting both. I pay homage to both. In that way, both are available to me in the work I do.

Stories from the past about the land, and stories from the city, go hand in hand. Stories from up home are still relevant right now and even to life in the city.

This old fulla up home was telling me about all the crazy whitefullas that go swimming all the time where there's crocodiles. It's like being in the city and walking across the traffic lights when they're green and getting hit by a truck. The crocodile is really smart. A lot of people think he's stupid. But I always say, he been round here for a million years and you don't get to be old by being stupid. He's doing something right because he's still here.

Some of the kids put up their hands and say, 'Monty,

do Aboriginal people wrestle with crocodiles?' 'No, only crazy white people do that.' 'Do crocodiles eat Aboriginal people?' 'Maybe, but where I come from they love to eat tourists best.'

One kid one time couldn't stop laughing. And I say, 'Well, us blackfullas, if we in there and we see one crocodile there, we go away from it. We don't turn round and say, "you want to punch up?", because we know who's gunna win. You don't worry about what they do on TV. No, you got to respect the crocodile.'

And that's what the old fulla was telling me. One time he was standing up on top of this hill and right down there was a nice big waterhole. 'It was a really beautiful waterhole,' he said. 'But round the corner you got some crocodile, a couple of ten-foot crocodile. That's where they live. And it's a really beautiful place, you know, salt-water place. And right in the middle you got about a dozen whitefullas in there swimmin'.'

The old fulla sings out to them and waves his arms, 'Hey! You fullas better get out of there. Big crocodile. He over there, he bin come and get you, you gotta look out, he bin livin' just round there. Get out now. He bin come and get you!'

And all them fullas in the middle, they turn around. They can't hear much. They just wave and say, 'Hello. It's beautiful in here, come on in.' The old fulla says, 'Good go! Stuff you! Get out of there. Crocodile over there!'

The old fulla was telling me a story about a couple of fullas that were taken. This bloke was in the water washing himself and the crocodile just took him. It's like, you don't really go in there, you know? If you go anywhere to someone else's land you gotta say, 'Is it okay to go here, or to go there, or what's this bush here, does that thing sting you?'

The crocodile could be drugs or alcohol. You get your strength by listening to your elders, your uncles and aunties, your mum and dad. For these students, I say to them, 'It is your teachers, they're your uncles and aunties now'. Sometimes they go, 'Oh, yuck!' But it's true. They spend so much time at school with their teachers.

If you think you know everything and you just go out and do it, that crocodile disguised as drugs or alcohol will eat you up and kill you. When you come face to face with that you've got to know how to deal with it. To know how to deal with it you have to listen to your elders to get the strength from them in your spirit and your heart to deal with it, to go around it, to go over it, to know about it. Sure you might go near the area but then you say, 'Eh, I'll come back this way.' Same as drugs. You might even have a taste of it but then say, 'Well, I shouldn't do that. That's no good for me.' When you get down and out, that's what you need, your strength. And that's where you get it from, from your elders, from their wisdom and advice. That's why they're older and wiser. They didn't get there from being stupid.

The kids ask me, did I go to school? Do my nieces and nephews go to school? And I say that they go to three schools. And they say, 'What do you mean?' 'Well, they go to Aboriginal school, that is, learning about their own culture, the songs, the dances, the stories from their area. Then, just like you, there's primary school and high school. Then there is another school that a lot of people don't see and that's learning to protect yourself from the police and negative reactions from the non-Aboriginal community.'

A lot of people ask why there are so many Aboriginal people in jail. An example of what happens is this. The police pull up beside you and call out things like, 'Your sister's a whore. We screwed her last night.' And they say terrible things about your mother. This happened not only when I was a teenager but I can remember as early as when I was nine or ten.

It still continues today, only instead of me it's my nieces and nephews that cop the brunt. They bait you until you react. So you react in the only way you know how, by answering them back, 'Get stuffed!' Then they say, 'Don't you get smart with me, you little . . . abo.' And you react some more. You don't even have to get physical. Just words are enough. So, they pick you up and take you down to the police station, the bullymen shop, and they give it to you.

It's a terrible feeling when you lose control of your bodily functions.

After about half a dozen times of this you say to yourself, 'Well, I'm doing the time, but I'm not doing the crime.' And so you think, stuff it, I might as well be getting something out of this. You don't get very far like that. So, this is the third school. Learning how to protect yourself from the authorities.

I go to lots of schools where a majority of the students have English as their second language. They can understand what I'm saying when I talk about schools outside school because they get taught another language at home and then they come to school and they get taught other things.

The mixture of teachers and their backgrounds with the mixture of students and their backgrounds is great. Anglo-Saxon to Greek to Indian . . . you name it. You walk into these culturally mixed schools and you never feel self-conscious walking around there. Some secondary schools you walk into don't have this mixture. You feel self-conscious and say to yourself, 'Oh, here it comes, abo, boong . . .' The influx of people from different cultural backgrounds has changed things.

Because of their strength within themselves from retaining their languages, songs and dances from whatever country their parents came from, I know these kids will understand. So I make this point. Being an Aboriginal person means having non-Aboriginal people give their version of your history. The recorded history about Australia only shows one side. The heroic deeds of white explorers, 'discovering' Australia, 'penetrating' a 'harsh, inhospitable land'. I read an article using this kind of description just the other day in a major Melbourne newspaper. They call the places where Aboriginal people were detained 'reserves' or 'missions'. But to us these places were concentration camps. In history books they talk about the 'settlement' of this vast land, Australia, as if it was vacant. In reality it was an invasion.

What the white people, the government, would do was take the strong people, the ones who stood up and spoke out, the ones they called 'trouble-makers', and put them on someone else's land, another tribe's land. That would break their spirit. When they were taken to land that wasn't their homeland they'd say, 'We can't dance here, we can't do anything here because we're on some-body else's land.' You see, that would help break their spirit. Dissension would start between the groups that had been brought in. Not only between themselves, but with the group whose land they were on. So that was a deliberate ploy of the government to break the spirit of our people.

In the area I grew up in, Palm Island was where they used to send all the 'uppity' Aboriginal people, the 'trouble-makers'. It became a penal settlement for convicted Aboriginals who were sent there for punishment. Traditionally, Palm Island is the land of the Munburra people. Today, Palm Islanders refer to themselves as Bulkamin, which means many groups. Families of the Munburra people still live there today.

When I'm in a culturally mixed school, I say, 'You imagine, how many groups of different backgrounds have we got here in this classroom? Imagine if your people were taken off their land and put on somebody else's land. What if we took a few of you from here and a few from over in this country and a few from . . . and we put you all together on someone else's land, what would you all do?' And they say, 'Probably kill each other.' I also stress that the people who have been shifted from their land to somebody else's land, especially within Aboriginal culture, lose their strength because your strength is from your land.

The same at Yarrabah; many nations were put together. On top of that there are many neighbouring groups as well. My cousin Bobby Patterson says of us Kunggandji people on Yarrabah, 'We are like a minority group on our own land now.'

About eight or nine years ago when I rang Mum she said there had been something like thirty deaths in the past month and a half on Palm Island. That's thirty funerals in just over one month in one Aboriginal community of about two thousand people. So many of those dying are young people like my niece Tania, who recently took her own life. She was nineteen. To understand why this is happening you have to understand the history that has led to this, you see.

It's all about replacing. Our beliefs are taken away and replaced with Christianity. We were told not to do our dances – our spiritual dances were replaced with barn-dancing and square-dancing. Our songs were replaced with hymns and folksongs from a different country. Foods. The traditional bush tucker was not allowed. We had to become reliant on whatever the overseers of the reserves dealt out to us. Sicknesses came about with the introduction of new diseases and the change of food. Name changing. Some people were given a different name every time they were moved. This confused their identity. When asked where they came from they didn't know any more. Alcohol. My cousin Gerry Fourmile says, 'Aboriginal people are the strongest people in the world. That alcohol takes away our strength. The strength of being with your spirit. You can't focus with that alcohol in you. That's why it is given to us.'

These deaths occur because of the dissension between the relocated groups and the original groups of that area, and of course everything that is caused by this replacing. So now you have the situation where alcoholism, fighting and suicides are the main killers of our people.

After Yarrabah was taken from the church and became a government reserve, the authorities wanted to put a pub there. The elders were against it but the government went ahead and set up the canteen. Not only that, they put it right on top of one of our sacred sites.

And still the question is always asked, 'Why do Aboriginal people get drunk all the time?' To this young girl this day, it was a very simple question. There was no malice in the way she asked. So, I explained in a way I thought she would understand.

'Well, there are lots of things that are misrepresented about Aboriginal people,' I said. 'Now, say if you are at this school, someone walked past you one day and you had your finger up your nose. You were picking your nose, digging around for a big booga. And these people walked past and they said, "Oh, yuck!". They went and made up this big poster along with this little newsletter and wrote, "So and so picks her nose, don't shake her hand, she's dirty, she's disgusting." And then they passed it all around the school so that when everybody sees you they go, "Yuck". No one would go near you. They put these letters out all the time about you picking your nose. Then you say to yourself, "Well, I s'pose everybody must pick their nose at least once in their lifetime, so there's nothing wrong with that." But everyone makes out it's such a bad thing and you're the only one that does it. Would you like that?' And this girl goes, 'No'. And I say, 'Well, that's the same as Aboriginal people. All you hear is about Aboriginal people getting drunk. So you see, you wouldn't like it just to hear about you picking your nose for boogas all the time. Aboriginal people feel the same about alcohol.'

Don't you think that's a good way of looking at it? A lot of people do drink and a lot of people do get drunk, black or white. Why put it on Aboriginal people? Alcohol is everybody's problem. We get all the attention for not handling our alcohol but then within the wider community of Australian society it is a far worse problem.

Just say there is a park bench with two destitute drunks sitting side by side. One of them is a whitefulla, shabbily dressed with a half-empty bottle of cheap wine. The other is a blackfulla dressed the same and he also has a cheap bottle of wine. Sitting side by side they are the same as each other. The difference is only in the eye of the passer-by. The whitefulla is down on his luck and homeless. He's had a few bad breaks, people think. But, to most people, the blackfulla represents his people, 'See, Aboriginal people just can't handle the drink.' They can't see what has happened to this blackfulla. The spirits of his ancestors have been replaced by the spirits in the bottle.

There are a lot of reasons why people drink, black or white. There are a lot of Aboriginal people with a lot of good reasons to drink.

The story of one of these parkies was told to me by my aunty. She saw him just before he died. He told her why he'd been drinking all of his life. You see, he was a stolen child. He was about five when the white people, the government authorities, came around to take him away from his mother. These men pack-raped his mother. He saw it all. After that he swore that when he got old enough he was going to kill every white person he could. But then, as he got older, he met some beautiful white people who took care of him and loved him. This confused him. So that he would not hurt any good white people he got drunk. He said to my aunty, 'I'm too frightened to be sober. I don't want to hurt any good whitefullas.' So that's why he stayed in that state of drunkenness all his life until the day he died. That was last year.

I had to be out at this school by eight-thirty, nine o'clock. It was an hour and a half from home. There was fog and it was freezing cold and I was late. I had to get changed in the toilet, and it was freezing. And then I had to walk back from there to the classroom with just my judda jah on. I walked in out of this cold, into an even colder place. That's what it was like. Walking from being in the North Pole to the South Pole. So, I walked in and I thought, 'Eh, look out.'

I could feel this negative energy zinging around the room and I knew I had to dig deep and stay strong in my heart. Some of the students were making jokes and snide remarks. You can feel these things hit you from all over the room – disbelief, giggling, whistling, you know. I imagine it's like being in the ring with Muhammad Ali or Mike Tyson. You come out and no matter how many times they hit you, you can't fall down because if you do they'll stick the boot in.

The punches kept coming, so, just after I'd started performing, I put my clapping sticks, my bibra, down and said, 'Well, okay. It's up to you fullas. I'm here for a reason. I'm just a human being who happens to be

Aboriginal.' I said, 'If you want to learn something, here's your chance. I don't know that much, but you can learn something about your own place.' I said, 'Some of you are going out into the big wide world next year and let me tell you, it's pretty tough out there. What you have to do before you get out there is find out about where you live. That's how you're going to be strong. If you don't have that then you'll be stuffed up even more. This is your chance. You've got to start here and now.'

And I said, 'If you want to stuff around, you can do that. I'll just put everything down and I'll tell you Dream-time stories and you're going to know stuff-all when I leave, 'cos you knew stuff-all when I came here.' And I said, 'I want to be here. I'm not angry at you, because you're the ones that are going to be the losers, not me. I don't want to come in here and bash you over the head with the Aboriginal flag. I don't want you running up the street with me shouting for Aboriginal land rights just because it's the thing to do. If you want to do that, that's fine, but I want you to listen and learn. Look at things. Look at these issues. I'm just who I am.'

Images of Aboriginal people have been processed through the media over long periods of time and they are hard to shatter. When you come to the Year 8 to 12s, a lot of the kids are really aware. And a lot of them are not. They haven't left themselves open to other influences. When they are given the chance to listen to another side of the story in a non-threatening way, they suck it up like a sponge.

You walk into some schools and they applaud you as soon as you walk in. Then you'll go to areas where it's not culturally mixed, the teachers call it WASP areas, White Anglo-Saxon Protestant areas. You'll know how hard you have to work just by walking into the room. There's this intensity of feeling, scepticism.

If I really want to bring in the big guns I say, 'When I was your age, I wasn't allowed to do these dances. I came from two reserves, Yarrabah and Palm Island. If you painted up and did a dance like this, they would strip you off and tie you to a tree and flog you. And then throw you in jail for one or two days on bread and water. Just for saying one word of your language. Just for doing one dance. So a lot of people have suffered and died for me to be able to keep this dance. Not only for me to keep it but for you to keep it too.'

After about five minutes on my soap box, I said to this class, 'Do you want me to go on?' They all nodded. Then I said, 'Well, the first dance is this. Why I want you to do these dances with me is because then you get involved in them and you walk away and say, "Well, heck, I can understand where he's coming from." If you get up and do dancing, it stays with you. If you sit down and watch, then that's good too, but then you've not really been involved.'

They all got up.

Afterwards I went into the staffroom and sat down. I was really drained. The cementing of this thing, this connection, it takes it out of you. Rather than saying,

'Stuff you, you bunch of white honkies', then leaving, you're saying, 'You really need to have this. You are the ones that really need to have this.' And you keep giving.

So, I was talking to the teachers afterwards and this one teacher sat down there right in front of me and she said, 'I don't know that you really know what you've done.' And I thought, 'Uh oh, what have I done?' And she said, 'No. You actually had them sitting down there for over an hour. None of the Year 12s in this school have ever done that before.' So, me and this teacher and another one and the principal, we sat there and we talked for an hour or more.

The principal said, 'Look, I'd like to get you here for a week. For a week in residence. We'd pay you whatever you wanted.' My head was going, 'Well, it'd be pretty tough doing a few shows each day for this mob.' And he said, 'No. I just want you to come in to speak with small groups in their classrooms, have a cup of tea and just sit there and talk to them like we're talking now.'

I looked at this man. I just loved him. He had this beautiful look on his face and sincerity came through his eyes from his heart. I felt good because he was really interested. The money thing wasn't an issue. Can you imagine being paid all this to walk in and sit down and have a cup of tea and just talk to the kids? I'd do that for nothing. He said, 'Our kids out here really need this. They need Aboriginal people to come out here and do this for them. Can we work something out?'

My mum, Dot Pryor

'The tears may have dried but you never stop grieving.'

My dad, Monty Pryor

*'I believe we are all one people. Everyone is a human being.
We've got to try and help each other.'*

My Aunty Val Stanley
*'When I am working with these young ones that are in trouble,
that's where I start. I start working on their sense of identity.'*

My Uncle Herbert Patterson and me
*He just looked at me and said, 'You Boori. I give you my name.
Boori means fire.'*

My Uncle Peter, language name Gullumbah, and Aunty
Milda Prior and me
'We were only black when they wanted us to be.'

My Aunty Alma and Uncle Henry Fourmile
'Most of my people, the Yidinji, stayed all together away from the
main misson and we could keep our culture going more that way.'

Me and my Aunty Pauline Fourmile
Whenever I go back to Yarrabah my Aunty Pauline makes a big fuss. She cries and runs to me, hugs and kisses me, and says, 'Oh my boy, where you bin?'

My sister Cilla Pryor
'Our parents really encouraged us to learn as much as we could at the white school even though Dad had only gone to Grade 4.'

Me and my sister Chrissy Winitana
Aunty said to me she saw her mother, Nanna Susie, sitting by the fire and warming her hands and rubbing little Chrissy all over as she spoke in Kunggandji language.

My sister Chicky Pryor
'Losing your child is like your last bit of breast milk being drained from you, and there is no more life left in your body.'

My sister Toni Pryor and Lawrence Masso
We laugh at situations, we laugh at ourselves, even at the saddest times. It's our way of surviving.

My cousin Gerry Fourmile, language name Quiblum
'Aboriginal people are the strongest people in the world.'

My cousin Henrietta
Fourmile
*She has always been a
great inspiration to me
with all the work she
has done in the
academic field for our
people.*

My cousin Paul Fourmile
and me
*'Us that are still alive, we got
that pain of fighting for our
survival all the time.'*

My cousin Bobby Patterson, language name Binjarrabi
'We are like a minority group on our own land.'

And I think that's what gives me spirit and strength. These beautiful people, like this person here.

I don't know what I call on in these intense situations. I know the strength comes from my brothers, my sister and my nephew. But I know it's also from my mum and dad and all the elders. I can't be weak. It really is a powerful feeling because it's like you know you have to run the 100 metres in X amount of seconds and keep running it for a whole hour. That's what it's like in these really intense ones.

I gave a talk up in the Blue Mountains, in New South Wales. It was a high school, the Year 11s and 12s. This one boy was sitting down and he had his arms folded. And he was really tense. He put up his hand and he said, 'Well, my mother worked in this Aboriginal organisation and she said they give Aboriginal people homes and they give Aboriginal people this and that. And then the Aboriginal people walk out of the homes and burn them down and then they live outside and then they whinge that they don't get anything.'

And I said, 'Can you tell me where that happened?' And he said, 'No'. And I said, 'Well, perhaps if you understood *where* it happened then you could understand *why* it happened.'

And I went on to explain, 'Possibly, it would have been in areas where there are fewer whitefullas, and the blackfullas are still living closer to their traditional ways. In the middle or up the Top End or out west. Or even up the top in Northern Queensland. As my brother always said, "It's just that city blacks have been raped longer than country blacks." In other words, Aboriginal people living in the city areas have become more used to white-fulla ways. You can't just walk into areas through the middle, where there are hardly any white people, and say, "We're going to build a house for you here. Here are the keys to the house and goodbye." These people are used to living a certain way, and that's not the way of the white people.'

What was in his eyes was what his mother had told him. He didn't know the circumstances or where it was. He kept looking angry. And I said, 'You're still not trying to understand. You're sitting there being angry and using up all this energy. You're wasting all that strength for what? For nothing. You're sitting down with your arms folded, looking at me, being angry at me. Why are you being angry at me? I don't know you. You seem like a nice bloke. I'm not angry at you. And I'm not angry at your mother either. All I'm angry at is that, when people tell you things like this, they don't explain the reasons why these things occur.'

It's like saying one group of young kids use knives and kill people and then you say, 'Oh, all teenagers are like that nowadays.' I didn't yell at him and say, 'You idiot!' All I tried to say was, 'have a think about it'. So he could look at it. Not me telling him, but presenting the issue in a way so that he could look at his anger himself.

Sometimes you don't know the anger is there until it's addressed. I was walking along the pathway during recess at this secondary school down in Tasmania. I heard these boys walking behind me saying, 'Hey, there's the abo.' I continued walking, then heard them say the word again. 'He must be the abo that's doing the dancing.' I tried to let it slide, but they continued. So I turned around and stopped them in their tracks. 'Hey, you fullas.' Two of them shot off in different directions and left one fulla standing there all by himself to face the music. What are friends for? Before I could get a word in, he babbled, 'Wasn't me. They said it. I didn't say anything.'

I fronted him and said, 'Do you know that word you just called me is a derogatory term?' His face paled. Then he got the guts up to say, 'What's a de . . . dero . . .? What's that mean?' He looked like I was going to tell him he'd said a deeply spiritual, sacred word and he was going to die. I could hardly keep a straight face. I said in the sternest voice I could muster, 'Just think about what you're saying. "Abo" is demeaning. I mean, a word that puts Aboriginal people down.' I had to rush around the corner 'cos I was cracking up laughing.

In this class, this young boy got up and asked in a really snide voice, 'How come you Aboriginal people are so slow? You don't progress yourselves, and you're lazy,

63

and you get drunk all the time.' Even in a situation where you expect a question like this, it still hits you like a bullet. I asked him, 'What's your name?' This is how I get my breathing space after a question like that. I get my composure so that I can answer him constructively and not just fight fire with fire.

You have to be the water to put out the fire. If you fight fire with fire, everything burns.

I went on, 'Let me ask you something. Can you speak an Aboriginal language?' He said, 'No.' 'Do you know any Aboriginal dances?' 'No.' 'Do you know any Aboriginal songs or stories?' 'No.' 'Have you read any books that Aboriginal people have written?' Every question I asked, he answered 'no'.

By now I'd cleared myself of my anger and I went on to say, 'I can speak your language. I can do your dances. I know your stories, I read your books. So, who is the slow one? Who is being lazy? Aboriginal people were forced to learn your ways. Here you are being offered a chance to learn. No one is forcing you. You must do this for yourself.'

One particular time I was at this school in Adelaide and I could feel this negativity from a few of them. It came to a point where messages were being sent but weren't being received, so I went in with the big guns. To explain where Aboriginal people are at today, I told them about the raping of women, the taking away of children, about a few of the massacres, about my brother dying . . . After I finished, my heart was hurting and I had tears in my eyes. I looked up and it was as if a bomb had hit the room. I even gave myself a fright. There was silence for about thirty seconds or more.

One girl in the third row was crying. She asked, 'How come you don't hate us white people?' I said, 'Well, it's not your fault all that happened. But it will be your fault if you don't listen and learn from the past. By learning from the past you can understand where Aboriginal people are at now. Anger and hate will destroy you.'

Another girl put up her hand and said, 'How can we help?' I said, 'Well, you are helping, by listening.' She put her head down and cried.

Sometimes, without even knowing it, the tough nuts help me get through to them. West of Melbourne, the Melton area has a pretty tough reputation. At one school, I dragged these two big tough-looking fullas up and got them to dance. They looked like they weren't into it at first. Then they were up for every dance. This teacher came up to me at the end and said, 'You know that tough one that wanted to dance all the time? Before you came out, he said, "Oh, Miss, I don't want to go. I don't want to learn anything about Aboriginal culture. Why should we learn about Aboriginal people? They never done anything for us." All of a sudden, he was out there doing the dance and you couldn't stop him!'

It's more a thing of protecting themselves, not wanting to be shown up or embarrassed in front of their peers and teachers for knowing very little, in this case, about Aboriginal people. By finding themselves in the right environment where they are safe to seek out that knowledge, they get involved.

It's the same as the questions you get about whether you are a 'real' Aborigine. A lot of the time I think it comes from people not being able to cope with facing their own ignorance. I think to myself, 'Well, if I'm not a real Aborigine, then how come I've lost my sister and two brothers through suicide and how come I lost my nephew through police harassment – that's not counting all the cousins and extended family who have gone before their time in the same way – and how come I got smashed up walking down the street after the coppers pulled me over and abused me? I'm black enough for all that.'

There was a question from this Year 8 kid halfway through a show: 'Are you a real Aborigine?' I just looked at him. And he pulled back into his shell. Sometimes you're asked questions like this to provoke a reaction. Other times, the same questions are asked because they really want to know.

This time, the young boy was genuine, so I had to become softer. He thought he'd said something wrong. I said, 'Well, if you ask a question and I don't understand it, I can't answer you. Why would you want to know if I was a real Aboriginal? How do you mean, am I real? Of course I'm real. I'm human and I'm standing in front of you and I just happen to be black. And I have paint on.' And he said, 'Are you an actor?' And I said, 'No, no. I know my Aboriginality and where I come from.'

He thought I was acting. So I could see where he was

coming from. In the past, migaloo actors, whitefulla actors, were painted up to play the parts of Aboriginal people because they didn't want black people to have any acting roles. That is, not unless it was for a situation like the Australia Day celebrations in 1938. Then a group of Aboriginal people were rounded up from the missions, trucked down to Sydney, and forced to take part in the re-enactment of the landing of the First Fleet from England. At the time, there were protests from a lot of Aboriginal people, but the re-enactment went ahead with a group of red-coated, white soldiers with fixed bayonets coming ashore and dispersing the unfriendly 'natives'.

I always explain my family groups and where I come from when I meet the students. Ten minutes into question time this day, a Year 10 student asked, 'Are you a full blood?' I love answering this way, 'Yes, I'm full of blood.' This way I find out if they're listening. I had explained my background earlier, so I went on and asked, 'Why would you ask that question?' He said that one teacher had told him you're not an Aboriginal unless you are a full blood. I put the ball back in his court and asked him what his background was. He said, 'Greek.' I said, 'That means, if you were to marry someone that wasn't Greek, when you had children, they wouldn't be Greek.' He said, 'Oh, yes they would.' So I said, 'Well, sit down because I think you just shot yourself in the foot.'

All that matters is to sit down and say hello and ask, 'Where do you come from?' If the person wants to say, 'Well, my mother is Aboriginal, my father is from Ireland

and I'm this one and that one . . .' then, that's fine. But to walk up and say, 'Hey, are you a full blood? What are you, a quarter caste, one-eight or one-sixth . . . or . . . ?' I get angry at that.

I say to myself, 'Why? Do you go up to a Chinese person and ask, "Are you full-blood Chinese?" Or an Italian, "Are you full-blood Italian?"' If you accept their nationality, then you should accept us for who we are. Otherwise where does it end, this concentration of halves and quarters and, besides, what does it matter? We've just got to get down to the truth that is beyond this smokescreen. And we've got to face the truth and ask questions.

People find ways to avoid facing the truth. There are usually three ways of thinking that people use to rid themselves of any guilt or responsibility for past actions. The first classic one is, 'We didn't do it. It happened two hundred years ago.' The second is, 'Well, you're not a full blood, anyway. If you are a full blood then you should be living out in the bush, not in the city.' The third is, 'Oh, you came from somewhere else anyway.' This assumption is based on white anthropological studies that say we walked across from Asia when the land mass was one. Why couldn't we have walked to the rest of the world from here? How far do we need to go back? What does it matter anyway whether we walked across from Asia or did some marathon swim?

We should be dealing with what is at hand by learning from the past, not using it to avoid facing the issues of today.

It's amazing what some teachers are doing in the schools to get their students to face these issues. Especially in the more affluent schools where the country's decision-makers will come from. I never imagined that I would be able to speak my words at any, what my mum would call, 'flash' schools.

This bloke Vince Toohey, my yubbah, which in my language means my brother, grew up in Armidale in country New South Wales. His mother was a primary school teacher and he says, right from the word go, she passed on to him the value in Aboriginal culture. He reckons she was the one who made him open-minded about Aboriginal issues. There was quite a big Aboriginal community where they lived. Later, when he went to boarding school, he remembers coming across a lot of really racist kids who came from the country as well. He didn't say anything because he thought he'd get his head bashed in, but when they used to mouth off about Aboriginal people, very ignorant things, he used to think, 'No, that's not true.' Eventually, when he came to teach in schools himself, he thought, 'Well, I'm in a position to change attitudes.' He has the view that even if it is one kid out of a classroom of thirty that he changes, then at least that is something.

The basic point Vince tells the kids is:

Don't go into an issue if you only know one point of view. You've got to know both sides of the issue to give a decent opinion of whatever it is. At the end of the day, you've got to know there's always two sides to every story. Don't be arrogant. Don't be ignorant. If you kids are going to kick on to be leaders and movers and shakers in the society, you can't be one of these narrow-minded morons. Get in and decide legislation and know that it has an impact on other people.

He tells them:

You've got Aborigines who have lived in this country for fifty to sixty thousand years without changing the environment that much, living off the land. And then you've got another culture that came along after the Industrial Revolution, and set up big cities with such rapid change to everything around. If the world keeps going the way it is, they say we've only got a hundred years or less to go of this unsustainable development. The world will be a polluted mess, or there will be mass starvation, or the weather patterns will be completely changed forever. That's not a successful culture. We're going to be just like the Romans who reached a peak and then dipped straight down.

I like how Vince brings in that perspective of history. He's a history teacher and he can put what is happening here now into a context of the patterns of what has gone on in other places before. Vince draws on examples from across the world. He asks his students the question, 'What is a successful culture?' He reckons most of them think western culture is the best because it's got these great scientists and it can make bombs, and people can zap around the world faster than the speed of sound.

He lets them go on and then brings in what David Suzuki, the Canadian environmentalist, points out: 'A successful culture is one that can sustain itself for a long time. One that can keep going.' That puts Aboriginal culture in a pretty strong position, don't you reckon?

That's what Vince tells his students. He impresses on them not to be so arrogant about thinking that western culture can keep going and going. Aboriginal culture survived all the way through the Egyptians, the Greeks, the Middle Ages up until now. He talks about white Australia only coming on the scene just after the Renaissance. He tells them that the real success story is the Australian Aborigines, who were the first here. I like that. He says:

The amazing thing is that they are still alive even after being shot and poisoned on a mass scale. They are still going. And another amazing thing is they're not really militant. They could have their own guerilla army and I would excuse them straight away because of the things that have happened to them. Somehow they keep going. They haven't got to the stage where they can't tolerate whites any more.

He ain't heavy, he's my brother!

I was in a very rich school in Adelaide. I'd just shared lots of personal stories about police harassment, deaths in the family and the ongoing mistreatment of Aboriginal people. One boy, they were Year 12s, asked me, 'How do we know you're telling the truth?' That's a good question. I began by saying, 'I'm not a politician. I'm not after your vote. I'm not preaching another religion in the hope of having you come to my flock. You'd probably tell me to flock off, anyway, if I did! I don't want your money, although you've paid for me to come and speak. The truth is I've heard stories, not only from my own family's experiences, but stories from the elders, which made me weep and made me scared in my heart. I know I tell you the truth because my parents live through the pain and deal with it. I am living through the pain and this is my way of dealing with it.' He came up to me after the talk and said, 'I know you're telling the truth. I hope you didn't mind me asking that question.'

Don't ever be scared to ask a question. It doesn't matter if it is demeaning, racist, silly, ignorant, stupid, any question at all. I will answer it truthfully and to the best of my knowledge. If you don't ask, you will never know.

It's the simplest thing. All anyone has to do is ask. The hardest thing, though, is to have the courage to stand up and ask a question.

A question is very different from a statement. Sometimes this will happen when someone is angry. They make a negative statement to provoke a negative reaction. The way to deal with that is not to become angry within yourself. You have to become soft like a pillow, so the anger has somewhere to land. Then eventually, the anger will peter out and not hurt itself or you.

Hard against hard means you just bruise each other. To be soft, you have to become bigger than the issue itself. My amazing mother does this all the time.

Like everything, in every field, there are people in the media who work very hard to find ways to bring out the true story. A friend of mine, James Valentine, was doing an interview with me for the Australian Broadcasting Commission. He came to tape some of my performance. I had three shows that day. The first show was full-on. There were close to a hundred and fifty, two hundred children in each show. It was in a canteen area, on a cement floor. The sides were open. That meant my voice drifted so I had to work extra hard. But the kids were so beautiful I couldn't stop, even though my body was saying, 'slow down a little bit'. After the next show, which was very intense, James said, 'Boy, you're still breathing.'

Then at the end of the third show he said, 'Hey, you're still alive!' I was exhausted.

The first time I heard myself in the interview was when it was played on air. I heard the introduction to the show and the didj playing. Then I heard myself telling the stories. I was stunned. It wasn't me talking. It was my brother Paul. And then I got a copy of the tape and sent it up to Mum and she said, 'Hey, that's Budda, eh?' And I said, 'No, that's me.' I had got really tired during the shows and all of a sudden I was talking like him. He was my voice. It was like he was pulling me up, he'd jumped in and said, 'Don't you dare stop now. Okay, brother, come on, let's go.' And I took a big breath and I kept going.

I am the driver of the vehicle but a lot of people jump on and push me. They push me along or pull me up. Sometimes I put too much into it, to making things better, and that's why I got so sick I nearly died a few months ago. I have to keep some space for me, too.

Even though I drive hundreds of kilometres a week all over the city – the other week I did six hundred kilometres – and you're doing two or three shows a day and I've been doing this for four years, I never get tired of working with children. In the wake of this beautiful reaction you see from all the students, I love telling these stories over and over again. Although the stories are the same, looking into the faces and hearts of a new group of children is like splashing cold water on your face on a hot day.

I protect myself with all these wonderful things I've been lucky enough to be given by children, not only from the little ones but right through to Year 12. The little ones paint pictures and send them to me and you see all the love, all the hearts and kisses they do for me, as well as beautiful drawings of the stories. The Year 10s and 12s write it all down. Those are their paintings.

I keep these gifts locked in my heart, inside me, inside here. Each one is really precious to have. So, when the anger comes at you and it's really powerful, for me, all I do is jump back inside. It's like being in a tent. I can remember this from the times I stayed out in the bush with my Uncle Peter and Aunty Milda in Happy Valley, a place where a lot of Aboriginal people camp in Townsville. They had a little shelter made out of corrugated iron. When the rain poured down heavy, it would beat down on the corrugated iron like thunder. You felt like it was going to fall in. You'd just wait there and all of a sudden it would ease off and slow down to a light rain, then clear up and the sun would shine. You'd walk out and you'd feel this steam coming off the ground and this wonderful smell and you'd feel nice and bright. Whereas ten, twenty minutes ago you were in this deluge of water and thunder and the world was falling in.

So, for me, the rain pouring down is the verbal abuse

and misapprehensions coming from people who have been ill-informed. That's the pounding on the corrugated iron. All I do is get inside myself in this little place where I keep the letters from the children, their drawings, and all their wonderful questions and thoughts. I get in there and have fun with all those things and that's my shelter. The way I'm talking about it, though, sounds like I'd take five days, but what I'm talking about happens in a second. It only takes me one or two seconds and I'm in there.

I always have this place inside my heart and all I do is jump in there, and when I come back out the sun is shining.

4

AWAY FROM HOME

You can't fall down. You fall down, you die.

I made the decision at a really young age not to drink, or smoke. I think I was six or seven when I decided I wasn't going to drink. Even then, I saw how my people hurt each other and sometimes died when they were lost through intoxication.

As I got older, I also decided I didn't have to take this oppression: on government reserves, the Queensland Act that was in force right up until 1971 dictated how every aspect of your social and economic life as an Aboriginal person was run.

When I was very young, we lived on the mission in Garbutt, the suburb of Townsville that was for blacks, fringe dwellers and poor whites who didn't have anywhere else to live. It was just called 'the other end' by everyone, even taxi drivers. It was not an officially gazetted reserve or mission, but after World War II the huts that had been occupied by the Air Force were taken over by the Department of Native Affairs, as it was known then, and became available as housing for the fringe dwellers like my mum and dad.

At a young age, I tried to find my strengths and weaknesses as a black person but, really, I didn't know what I was looking for. After failing my leaving certificate, I found myself being a brickie's labourer, a job my dad had organised through his friends in the building industry. I'd worked in lots of jobs going through school, mainly during the holidays. My older sister Sue was secretary at a soft-drink factory. I worked there packing the crates.

Some holidays I went down to Ayr, a small town on the Burdekin River, an hour's drive south of Townsville. I stayed with my Aunty Norma and I worked stripping sugarcane. I'd get up at four in the morning to be out in the sugarcane fields by five. I think I was about fourteen then. When I was sixteen I worked in the Ross River Meatworks, separating the hearts and the kidneys of slaughtered animals and putting them down the chutes. I remember riding home with my clothes soaked in blood every day. Earlier than this, when I was about seven or eight, my mum used to get me up at five every morning to water the garden. So, you can see, although I didn't leap for joy about doing these jobs, I wasn't afraid of hard work.

When it came to brickie's labouring, everything was

78

bearable – pushing the heavy barrows of cement up trestles, the carting of bricks, the sun and the sweat – but what I couldn't bear was the sound of the metal trowel smoothing the wet cement after the bricks had been laid. It makes my hair stand up on end even now. After a few months, I left. Pops ribs me about it even now. He says to people, 'Yeah, his first real job was too tough for him. He had to go back to school.' That's when I start to dig up anecdotes from the past about him, like when he used to strum his guitar and sing love songs to Mum in the kitchen while she was trying to cook. I have the pictures to prove it.

When I went back to school, I worked really hard to get my pass. I wanted to be an electrician when I left. I was eighteen. I applied to lots of places for an apprenticeship. They were all nice and sweet when I phoned to line up an appointment. But then when I walked in, they always told me the position was filled. At one place, I saw a migaloo mate of mine from school at the interview. We sat down after and had a chat. They'd given him the job but he hadn't even passed his final year at school.

My older sister Cilla is now Assistant General Manager of the Townsville Aboriginal Islander Media Association, which runs the radio station, 4K1G, and a video production unit. She describes how it was for her when she first left school:

In my time, the expectations of having an education weren't there. It was like a policy that Murris only needed to know how to read and write, nothing else. This is the 1950s and 1960s I'm talking about. The norm was that you went to Grade 8 and then went into domestic work if you were a girl, and labouring for the boys, that was it. In our family, our parents really encouraged us to learn as much as we could at the white school even though Dad had only gone to Grade 4.

I did Commercial Studies hoping to be a secretary and came through with As and Bs. It was very, very disheartening then when I applied for job after job and it was quite evident that it was only because I was black that I didn't get the jobs. Other kids that had flunked were getting jobs all around me. There wasn't the unemployment that there is now, so there were plenty of jobs available. Eventually, I left home and joined the Air Force just to get a job.

Because I had my driver's licence, I applied to a company called Cable Makers. They advertised for a driver-cum-storeman. I got the job. That was my first job after I finished school. After a while, I got this feeling that there was something more to do than driving a truck. Not that there is anything wrong with truck driving. Cable Makers was good and the boss was fantastic. All my co-workers treated me with respect. But there was something in me that made me move on. The options in Townsville were closed because of the colour of my skin.

Townsville is named after Robert Towns, the slave trader – that speaks for itself. The town was set up as a shipping port and quickly became the trading centre for all this northern region. Dalrymple's Hotel, one of the main hotels in the town, is named after a white man who was known for killing Aboriginal people. Townsville was one of the first areas around here to be cleared of Aboriginals. Most of the Wulgurukabba people, the traditional people from here, were exterminated like unwanted pests. Whoever was left was sent to reserves even as far away as Cherbourg in southern Queensland. Very few of the Aboriginal people in Townsville today are from this place originally.

I find it hard to drive around and see all the white-man's names for places over our significant sites. And I mean white man because they're almost always the names of white men. It's even more painful to see derogatory names like Black Gin Creek and so on. This is like calling a creek 'White Slut Creek'. Imagine naming streets in a Jewish area 'Hitler Drive' or 'Goebbels Court'. This is what it is like to live where placenames have been changed to be called after white people who have done the most appalling things to black people.

The overtones of the past still hover over the town. To be treated equally and given a chance to prove your capabilities as a hard worker is what my father has fought for all his life. A lot of that he has given to me. That's why I wanted a say in what direction my life went. Being Aboriginal, I couldn't do that in Townsville.

My sister Cilla was already in the Air Force at Wagga Wagga, New South Wales, and a few of my friends were going to join up, so it was a way out. I think there have been lots of things missing from my life which I could do nothing about because of having to leave home. It was very hard to leave everyone even though I knew I had to go to survive. I was only eighteen or nineteen and I was a skinny little blackfulla going all the way down to Adelaide. It was hard, not so much to deal with it, but to comprehend what I was doing and why.

Looking back, I think it's funny that the last thing in my mind when I joined the services was fighting for Queen and Country. That's not to say I wouldn't fight for this land. It was the same with most people I came across. They had their own reasons for joining which weren't often to do with patriotism. More often than not they signed the dotted line just to get a job. And that amazed me, too. Some of the blokes I met in the Air Force couldn't read or write. Being a blackfulla from the bush up in Queensland, I never imagined I'd come across any whitefullas that couldn't read or write.

The rookies camp at Edinburgh air base in Adelaide, where I first went, was a great learning experience and started me off on the road to where I am now. It was the first time I had been somewhere so cold that when you breathed steam came out. First time I'd seen that. I got off the plane in a nylon shirt and froze. Even though in my outfit there were mainly white Australians, with only one other blackfulla from up near Winton, the fact that we were all rookies levelled the playing field, so I felt quite accepted as an equal. When everyone is treated like cow manure, or something that gets stuck on the bottom of your sergeant's boot, then no one worries about what colour the cow manure is.

I was excited being out on my own for the first time and the comradeship between us rookies was tight. I got protected within the structure of the Air Force. I made some really good friends and it gave me time to develop. It would have been much harder if I'd just got on a bus and gone to a big city down south with nothing. Aboriginal people had their own areas within Melbourne, Sydney and Adelaide. They were very protective when outsiders appeared on the scene – black or white.

We were the same up home. That was back in the sixties when you really had to watch yourself, especially in the bigger cities. The police were more openly racist in those days. People could walk up and call you 'abo', 'boong', 'nigger', to your face and nothing could be done about it. You either had to fight or walk away. In the case of police, any reaction would mean you ended up in the lock-up on any charge they wanted to make up at the time, 'abusive language', 'resisting arrest' . . . That gave them the leverage to provoke you even more till you ended up in the Big House sentenced with assaulting police and so on. So, the Air Force was more or less a safe house for me until I found my feet.

Once again what I had learned from sport when I was younger held me in good stead for the new direction I was taking in my life. I started playing football at the Air Force base at Point Cook, Victoria. Andrew Richards, a local lad from Healesville, was a framie, an aircraft mechanic on the base. He was a mate of mine, a migaloo bloke. He was a very tall man, about two metres, and he could run fast and kick the football. He was just a lovely, lovely man. I ended up being best man at his wedding. He and I could write another book about all the mischief we got up to on and off the base.

Anyway, Hawthorn Football Club came out and saw us play and wanted both of us try out for the Reserves in the hope of playing senior-level football. When they came and picked us up, I was really scared because we were off to the famous Glenferrie Oval and I hadn't trained that much. I had a run there once and I left and I never went back again. They were interested in signing me up and they wanted me to come to training nights. Andrew went in and he ended up playing Victorian Football Association.

But I didn't feel confident within myself. When I met everyone, they were big, muscly fullas like Don Scott. Great tough footballers who did weights. I hadn't lifted a weight in my life. 'They'll kill me, these fullas,' I thought. And I hadn't been down there long and everything was still looking a bit strange. There was the great Aboriginal footballer Polly Farmer, who played for Geelong, and Siddy Jackson was playing for Carlton. A fulla from up home, Stevie Lampton, came down around the same time as me but that was it for Aboriginal players. I didn't

know any other blackfullas down there at the time so trying to hook up with anyone was pretty hard. So, I felt at
a bit of a loss and thought I'd just stay on the base.

I could still be in the Air Force, but I left because I
knew if I stayed I would be defeating the purpose I'd
moved away from home for. The reason I left home in
the first place was to find my strengths and learn something about myself and my capabilities. I knew I could
survive in the bush amongst my own people and feel at
home, but living within the city, within the white society,
I had to learn how to do that, too. Staying in the Air
Force I realised I wasn't really learning that. In the Air
Force you didn't have to think for yourself. So, after six
years, I declined the option to re-enlist for a further four
years and signed my discharge papers.

From the runway to the catwalk was an unexpected
step. I was still in the Air Force when I decided to do
these dance classes. I thought they'd help my basketball
skills. I saw this bloke dance at a night club. His name
was Antonio Rodrigues; he was Brazilian and taught all
kinds of dance – classical, modern, South American, jazz,
African, everything. So I went along to his classes. One
night someone said to me at the class, 'Why don't you try
modelling?' I said, 'Get lost', 'cos my mind thought of all
my sisters and brothers and relations giving me heaps:
'Hey, look out, who this fulla think he is?'

After a couple of weeks, I thought, well, it won't hurt
to go and have a look, and besides, they can only say no.
I walked into a modelling agency and had a talk. They

took some photos and made up a composite and I started to get work. Mainly catwalk work and promotions.

I was doing a promotion at the Royal Exhibition Building in Melbourne and one of the organisers raced up and asked me if I wanted to be a DJ. I said, 'What? I'm flat out dealing with what I'm doing here now.' I suppose my first reaction was the same as when I was asked to give modelling a go. But I love music. Eventually, I thought, well, the water might be deep but I can swim. So, I dived in head first.

I went over to a place called the Albion Charles Hotel in Northcote, Melbourne, just to have a look. This was where the man who had approached me at the modelling job worked as a DJ. He got me up behind the console to get a feel of things. The console was on the stage and the room was cosy. I listened to the music and watched people dance. I felt good. I suppose me standing up there, black and with the small afro I'd started to grow, people didn't think I was out of place either.

After that first night I started listening to the radio for presentation and speech patterns and tried to work on a style that would suit me. I sat down with a tape-recorder and practised and practised and practised until I wasn't scared any more about speaking or projecting my voice. Love of the music was never a problem because that came to me way back when I was a kid.

Pops used to listen to lots of country and western music. He could play harmonica, guitar and croon a bit. That's probably how he wooed my mum. As I said before, he used to sing to Mum in the kitchen after a few quiet ales. Hearing Hank Williams or Patsy Cline always brings back good memories of us all sitting around the Christmas tree unwrapping presents in 40° heat. Mum was a deadly singer too and played guitar. Mum, with her four sisters – Aunty Val, Aunty Norma, Aunty Glad and Aunty Audrey – formed a singing group called The Stell Sisters. Stell was my mother's maiden name.

I think most Aboriginal people then were brought up on a good diet of country and western music. The sixties with the Motown sound, Elvis, and my favourite group, the fab four, the Beatles, were my teenage years. I used to sit on the kitchen sink at our house at 266a Ingham Road, Garbutt on any of the Saturday nights that we didn't go bush, and listen to the radio. It didn't look too much like a radio. It had no cover, you could see all the little bulbs flashing and you had to be careful about touching it because you could be electrocuted, but it worked. It was one we found down the dump.

When the opportunity came to play music and get paid for it, I couldn't believe my luck. It felt great to be standing up there playing some of the music I'd listened to on the kitchen sink as a teenager. After about a month or so of getting up with the DJ at the Albion Charles and doing a bit myself, I could do a whole night alone. Although the hotel had a reputation for being a blood-bath and a rough-house, and there were times, lots of times, when there were fights and some people got shot, it was a safe place for me because of the music. People respected my feeling for the music that I was playing for them.

Plenty of blackfullas went there. People from all different backgrounds went there, too – Italian, Lebanese, Greek, Yugoslav . . . I ended up making lots of good friends. People always put their differences aside to enjoy the music. No one ever laid a hand on me because I was the person who was there to help people forget their troubles for at least a night. If Collingwood footy team lost, I'd have to dry their tears with music; the place was Collingwood crazy. If you barracked for another club, you had to watch yourself.

If a lot of them were out of work, I'd have to soothe their pain and make sure they got a couple of bottles of bubbly. The blackfullas would come up to me and say, 'Anyone give you trouble, you see us.' And the Italians would come up and say, 'Anyone give you trouble, you come and see us.' And so on, because they all needed that place to go to. It was rough and ready but there was an indescribable warmth there and I felt safe.

My mother and father came to the pub and saw me work one night. They were in Melbourne for a convention. One of the managers at the Albion Charles was a crazy Italian who decided it was in everyone's best interest to have this huge sign in lights at the front of the hotel which read, 'Friday and Saturday nights, featuring Monty, The Black Superman'. My mum took a photo of the sign and warned me if ever I gave her any trouble she would show it to everyone back home. My mother always has the last say. The word went out that my mum and dad were coming, so everyone behaved that night. They made up for it the next night.

Nightclubbing was just taking off when I started working at the Albion Charles. After two years, I moved on to work in most of the top nightclubs in Melbourne. It was the time of the Bee Gees, 'Saturday Night Fever' with John Travolta, Tina Turner with 'Nutbush', doing the Bus Stop with the Fatback band, flashing lights, smoke – boy, was there smoke – and doing your best, solo or in groups, to attract attention on the dance floor. I worked thirteen years DJing.

Working in the nightclubs, it's bums on seats and bar takings that count. A full house that is not drinking is no good for the management, your boss, the one that pays you. Also in the back of your mind you have to remember that the people coming in through the door pay your wage. You have to work the crowd through music so that they want to drink. They have to go willingly and feel good about being led to the waterhole. Don't you think it's ironic that I was getting paid to make white people drink?

New Year's Eve is the one night when I let my hair down. Everyone gets drunk on New Year's Eve and I wasn't going to be left out. There's some great stories that my good friend and DJ Allan Knights could tell about getting charged up on New Year's Eve.

My brother Paul came in the New Year's Eve before he died. It was a fancy-dress night. He walked in with just his judda jah on and all painted up. I didn't know he was coming in. I was just cueing up a record. I turned around and there was this didjeridoo stuck in my face. Everyone in the place thought it was the best costume. I kept saying through the night, 'It's not a costume, it's real.' He danced and played the didj for Happy New Year. People loved it, especially my mate Allan. Although he had just met Paul, he thought he was the greatest thing since sliced bread. I think it was the first time he'd met anybody who was louder than him and could tell longer stories.

Not long after that, Budda Paul died. I had time off from Lazars, a couple of months. When I came back, one of the regulars told me how he was really sorry about my brother dying. He'd been coming in for years and we'd talk. He said to me, 'Hey, Mont, I hope you don't mind me saying this, but I never knew you were black.' Straightaway I thought, gee, I know it's dark in here but there's enough light for me to see you. How come you can't see me? I knew what he meant though, he just saw me as Monty. The first time he saw me as an Aboriginal was when he read the news about my brother's death in the paper.

Other DJs I knew used to get drunk or stoned or both just about every night, but I knew that what was okay for them was not okay for me, being Aboriginal. There was a double standard that meant I had to be squeaky clean. If, just once, I had done what some of the other jocks did all the time, it would have been, 'See ya'. I could tell some management were watching for me to trip up but I never did and the crowds kept coming so they couldn't get rid of me. There were lots of DJs who wanted my job. Some were friends of the management. It was really competitive. The standards I set myself and the disciplined way I approached my work were to satisfy myself, not to satisfy anyone else. My work spoke for itself.

I felt good about working within the music industry because it had nothing to do with being funded through an Aboriginal organisation. White people are always putting Aboriginal people down for taking what they perceive as 'handouts' and apparently misusing tax payers' money. I always felt angry about having to justify getting government money for us to, as they say, 're-adjust'. Of course I believe money should be given to begin to heal a wound that is so deep, but, personally, I swore I would try my best never to put myself in a situation where I would become dependent on anything to do with government money, including the dole, no matter how hard I had to work.

There is this big build-up of anger about Aboriginal people supposedly getting things for free. A lot of people say, 'Well, my family are migrants. We came out here and worked really hard to build this country. We didn't get anything for free.' And I say, 'Sure, that's true. That's what this country is about. Your family has worked hard. But at least they got paid. My people never got paid when they worked for the whitefulla to build this country! People talk about the great white explorers that found their way across this country. Who showed them the way? Who cleared the land and broke in the horses?

Who did the work that white people didn't want to do? Black women cooked and cleaned and lots more . . . And all this for no pay.'

What most non-Aboriginal people don't know is that thousands of my people worked for ten, thirty, some of them sixty years and got nothing because all their wages were taken from them and put into a trust fund. My father worked for eight years with no pay. He worked on the cattle stations and cutting sugarcane. Like all Aboriginal people at that time, sometimes half, sometimes the whole of his wages went into the Welfare Fund or the Aboriginal Trust Fund, as it became known. If the station owner supplied your food and clothing, then the whole of your wage except for a small amount of 'pocket money' was put in the trust fund. If you lived elsewhere and had to pay rent and buy your own food, then only half your wage was put in the fund.

My dad was given his food to eat on the wood pile. To this day he has not been paid the money that was held for him 'in trust'. He is one of thousands of our people who worked for the whitefulla for years for nothing. Now, as my father and many others try to trace where this money has gone, they are frustrated at every turn by a bureaucracy that has a surprising ability to lose records and misplace millions of hard-earned dollars owed to black people.

Even today, the majority of Australians, the very ones who mouth off about the special treatment Aboriginal people are given by the government, don't know about this. The compulsory deduction from Aboriginals' wages started way back in the 1880s when the system forcing Aboriginal people onto reserves was set up. It was kept up for all Aboriginal people, wherever they worked, until 1965. If you were from one of the reserves, then this holding of your wages in trust was still going on right up until 1971.

The only way my father started to get paid a full wage for working before 1971 was by changing his name and saying he was from Ingham, not Palm Island Reserve. In those days you had to have an exemption ticket – a dog tag we used to call it – to be able to leave the reserves and be free to travel and work where you wanted like any other Australian.

You see, we weren't even regarded as Australians until the 1967 Referendum. Migrants to this country were regarded as Australians and could vote long before Aboriginal people were regarded as citizens of our own country, according to the white invaders. Isn't that amazing?

So, you can see that I was pleased to be earning my living on the strengths of my own abilities and getting paid for it in a mainstream industry when I was DJing. Although DJing in clubs was regarded as a 'black thing to do', 'black' meant black American. So, I grew myself an afro, a 'fro to go. An American friend of mine said I should call it an 'astro'. He also said, tongue in cheek, that I was the best Aboriginal basketball player he'd ever seen. Then he whispered, 'I won't tell anyone you're the only Aboriginal basketball player I've ever seen!' I never came across any other Aboriginal DJs. My Aboriginality never came into it until I went to Perth.

I was working at a nightclub in Melbourne. It was the place to go for funk, reggae, for black music. One of the owners asked me if I'd like to go and work in Perth. He co-owned a place over there and they were looking for a black DJ with a good collection of music, who could talk and dance and mix. I'd never been to Perth and I thought it would be great, so I said yes.

I rang the management at the nightclub in Perth. I sent over a résumé and a tape of my work. From our phone conversations, they were impressed with all the music that I had in my collection. After about three weeks of negotiations, the deal looked really good so I flew over for the re-opening of the club. When I got off the plane I was greeted by the manager and a black DJ from Hawaii. We went to the club, which was still being renovated. After lunch I played a bit of basketball with the other two DJs, then we had a big meeting with the owners.

We were all seated round this big table and one of the owners said to me, 'We have a bit of a problem here.' I said, 'What problem?' He said, 'We wanted somebody black.' I thought to myself, 'How black is black?' Then he continued by saying, 'We knew you were black but we didn't know you were an Aboriginal.' So? I thought. Then he said, 'Well, if we had you working here we'd have all the Aboriginals coming in.' He went on to explain about how they once had a Chinese cook and all the Chinese kept coming in, so they had to dish him. He said that the last thing they wanted now was a bunch of blackfullas in their nightclub. As if I'd be bringing in my mates in their judda jahs and we'd be throwing spears round the dance floor.

I looked across the table and one of the DJs that was from Hawaii was almost as dark as me. In their eyes, that was okay. So, I could have been black Indian, black Samoan, black anything, as long as I wasn't black Aboriginal. I was the right colour but I was the wrong race. The owner finished by saying, 'We'll pay you out but we can't have you working here.'

I didn't hit anybody. I didn't smash anything. I just got up from the table and walked out, back to my hotel room.

I rang Mum and Dad. My father was friends with someone who was head of the Human Rights Commission in Canberra. He rang them. The next day I packed my bags and records and caught the plane back to Melbourne. I was pretty devastated because I had cancelled all my work back there, sold my car and moved out of my house. I felt pretty stuffed up in my mind. I couldn't come to grips with the fact that it wasn't my colour now, it was my race. This took racism to another level.

Through my work as a DJ, I'd earned myself a good reputation. I knew I was good at what I did. Then I get this thrown in my face. I felt humiliated and rejected. I had trouble getting myself back together and dealing with these emotions when I was back in Melbourne. I started having trouble sleeping. My friend Mari suggested counselling. I said, 'Good go! I'm not going to see a shrink. Finding one who could understand where I'm coming from would be like finding a needle in haystack.' I'm happy to say, I found the needle in the form of an amazing woman who had survived the holocaust. We simply sat and talked and I felt safe sharing my pain with her.

The long and the short of it is that with the Human Rights Commission and a Melbourne lawyer and friend of mine, Ian Mawson, we formed a case against this club. The club was already known for its bad dealings, but this gave the Commission a case they could really sink their teeth into. Over a period of a year and a half there were negotiations with the club. Dame Roma Mitchell was the mediator. This is a woman you don't mess with.

Eventually, the nightclub owners coughed up a lot of money and made a personal apology. At the time, it was the biggest payout for any compensation in the history of the Human Rights Commission. For me, as well as my family, and I suppose for other Aboriginal people, this was one fight in the continuing war that we won. It was really big. The odds seemed stacked against us. But we stood up and dared to challenge our oppressor, and we won.

There was a lot of media coverage of this case around Australia. The one article I will never live down appeared in my own home town. My mother, being my mother, when asked to supply a photo of her son to be published with the article about the case, gave them a photo of me modelling with my afro. I had a great big grin across my face and I was lying back in these designer jeans, which is not really the image of a tough, take-no-prisoners black activist. She proudly sent me a clipping in the mail. I rang her up straightaway and said, 'How could you do this? How could you do this to your son?' She's going, 'What? What?' In the photo I look like a real poser. I could imagine a lot of my friends from school, who would have been wondering what I'm doing down south, picking up the paper and saying, 'Oh, he's turned into a wanker now!' My mum said, 'Oh, you look so beautiful, my son. That's a good photo of you.' With the giving of this one photo to the local paper, Mum paid me back tenfold for any mischief I'd got up to in my younger years.

Without those years as a DJ, I know I wouldn't be doing what I'm doing now. It taught me a lot about people and, more importantly, it taught me a lot about myself in dealing with people. Working a crowd in the nightclubs, you get to see people exposing all their vulnerabilities and shortcomings. More than anything, I learnt to respect other people for what they are no matter what their failings. I also learnt how to read people and know what they need and how to shift their moods around. I learnt how to quell their anger with music.

And that's what I still do performing now. I quell the anger in people, only now I use my own culture to do this: Aboriginal stories and songs and dances. When I tell these stories I can feel how it is music to their ears, music to ears that have been deaf for years and years.

It's been a long journey to where I am now. You have to go through a lot of mental anguish and a lot of physical pain on the way. Mental pain is a lot different from physical pain. It's a lot more destructive. Just say someone walks up and punches you in the face. Okay, you might go down and you might be hurt, but it doesn't take long for your body to heal. But inside, in your head and in your heart, it is really hard to heal.

You can't put a bandaid on your heart. The only thing you can do to stay alive is to give your heart a transfusion, and that has to come from your own people. That gives you the power to heal within yourself.

Knowing the strength of the past is the healing water. Yet, having been told for so many years that the strength of the past is not really yours, then it takes you a long time to turn it around and say, 'No, that is mine. The strength of this culture that is this land and that I am a part of, is mine.' And that is the only thing that can heal you when you come up against this mental hurt.

Now that I truly know that strength is mine to have, I am ready to receive it. When I made the decision to move away from home, I put the gaining of more knowledge of my own culture on hold. It hurt me to do that. It still hurts now.

So, that is what I am doing each time I go back home – learning. From my heart and from my soul I am still connected to home. Now I am asking things of my elders that I was afraid to ask before. When you leave they think that you have abandoned them. Maybe they think you've turned white. Well, I haven't, I've just learnt to survive in the white world without losing sight of where I come from. That puts me in a position to have some input into the changing of attitudes.

I'm just a grain of sand in this land we call Australia. All I'm trying to do is my little bit. What I do in schools is not about me as an individual person. It is about all the people who surround me and all the people who have died before me and all the people before them who fought hard, people I don't even know.

What I would like to see happen, within the school system, is that in each school, in each town, in every part of this country, space is put aside, a special room, dedicated to the local Aboriginal people. The first thing to be placed in it would be a map of Australia which details every Aboriginal group across the land. The first of these maps was done by Norman Tindale in 1974.

Then there should be another map which details all the Aboriginal groups, family groups and language groups within the state in which that school is located. Then another map pinpointing the suburb or area where the school is situated.

Once that is done, members of the local Aboriginal group should be asked to come in to teach the history of the area and local language words for instruments, bush medicine, food, stories, dances, songs, animals. In some areas, this valuable information was lost when this country was first invaded. But even in the middle of the most populated areas of this country, big cities like Melbourne, knowledge of Aboriginal history and present-day practice is available. In these city areas there are systems of elders in place which are strong and respected and which still work.

After these classrooms have been established, more things will be added as time goes on – paintings, stories, photographs, crafts. It's a hands-on experience for all the children who are at that particular school. By the time they leave school they will have knowledge of their own Dreaming area. That will make them feel more like they belong rather than being alienated through lack of knowledge. The same for the local Aboriginal people. Their pride will be returned through their culture being valued and respected.

Finding out is as easy as asking. A very beautiful friend of mine, Tom Mae, who is now the Secondary Curriculum Adviser for Catholic Education in Sydney did just that – asked. In 1993, when he was a teacher, he organised for seventeen hundred students from kindergarten to Year 12, representing fourteen different schools, to come together. Then he invited one hundred members of the Aboriginal community, too. He organised forty workshops on the one day. They included topics like the Dreaming, spirituality, storytelling, creative writing, technology, foods, medication, local Aboriginal history and culture, sport, personal experiences, black deaths in custody, land rights, reconciliation, social justice, and NAIDOC, National Aboriginal and Islander Observance Committee. As Tom said, he wanted everyone there that day, 'to talk, to learn and to recognise the dignity of each person'.

Walking in that day was an amazing feeling. With one hundred other blackfullas spread out across the school I was in my element. I caught up with lots of people I hadn't seen in a long time, like Mum Shirl, one of the most respected elders in the Aboriginal community; the Mundine family, a big sporting family; and George Bracken, one of the greatest Aboriginal fighters ever. The last time I'd seen George was in the mid-sixties in his brand new Valiant after he'd won a title. Having that many Aboriginal people in one place sharing their experiences was a huge event.

Schools could create links with Aboriginal communities in other parts of the country. An understanding of the differences between Aboriginal groups from different areas could be appreciated through building this communication system across the country. Imagine one day having a school trip to your brother or sister community in North Queensland or down in Tasmania, or in the Kimberley, or in the middle of Australia? Wouldn't it be great if schools could have a welcoming at assembly each morning in the traditional language of the Aboriginal people from their area?

Many Aboriginal communities across the country are

reviving their language and cultural ways. My cousin Renata Prior is working tirelessly reviving the Birri-gubba language. Together with others, she has produced a language kit and is now writing new songs using the old language. One of these songs goes:

I learnt the whiteman's words today
I read their books through and through
They're saying our Birri-gubba ways are gone
They say that we're all through
And our culture is all dead
But did they ever bother to ask you or me?

Reclaim this land your mother's land
Reclaim the blood that's in your veins
Reclaim this land for this is your home
Your ancestors wait for you to make your stand

Imagine if a lot of adults you meet, if they had learnt about these kinds of things in schools, they wouldn't have to be walking around in a state of ignorance still. I was in the newsagents one day, checking to see if I'd won anything on Tattslotto. This bloke is standing at the counter calling out to me, 'Hey, mate, you're a millionaire!' And I said, 'Not yet. I'm waiting for this bloke,' pointing at the owner, 'to tell me I've won.' But he kept going on saying, 'Well, you could go and get Victoria back. That's yours.' It was around the time when there was a lot of discussion in the media about Mabo and the emerging Native Title Act. I said, 'Well, no. This land is not mine.' He said, 'Yes it is. You're an Aborigine aren't you?' And I said, 'Yes, but this is Wurundjeri land. I'm a Murri, I'm from Queensland.' 'Oh.' There was silence. That gets back to the grass roots. There is a very basic level of ignorance about Aboriginal people that leads to a lot of fears and misconceptions.

The sorry thing is that it's often not until white people are outside this country that their lack of knowledge is exposed. This Year 12 student told me how she had spent time overseas with her parents. She went to school for a short time in America. Overseas students in that school had to give a paper on the history of the country they came from. When it was her turn, she stood up and started giving all the information about how Captain Cook discovered Australia and everything to do with the white history of Australia.

After a couple of minutes, students interjected, wanting to know if there were any indigenous people in her country and what she knew about them. She said all she could really talk about were the bad images, the suicidal, drunken, lazy, lost images. She said she was really embarrassed. When she came back home she made it a point to learn more about the black history of her country.

On the other hand, we have trainee teachers coming to this country who are given the job of teaching about Aboriginal culture in their first practice round. I met these three Canadian trainee teachers. Eventually, they came up home with me to the Laura Festival, this Aboriginal

Dance and Cultural Festival in far north Queensland, because they were so keen to learn about the culture of this land. One of them, Maria Caril, was put in the situation of teaching Aboriginal Studies on her first teaching round. She told me:

I knew as much about Aboriginal Studies as I did about landing on the moon. 'I'm teaching this?' I looked at the supervisor and I said, 'You realise I'm from Canada? You realise I have absolutely no background to this whatsoever? I haven't even taken a course here.' For three weeks I had to teach this. Student teaching. He said, 'Oh, that's all right. You probably know as much about it as we do.' That's what he said. He said, 'It will tell you in the book. Just follow the book. That's what we do.'

I go into the class and I'm teaching Aboriginal Studies. And I'm looking up the book in front of the class, 'And a woomera is? Anybody?' I'm reading it as I'm asking the question. 'What does Dreamtime mean?' I had no clue. I was reading the night before trying to figure it out. What's Dreamtime? What does it mean? And Terra Nullius. The book for the syllabus would give you a definition, but what does it really mean? What does it really mean to say this was an empty land?

It's what people haven't been told that harms this country. What they haven't been told is that there is a great

104

deal of Aboriginal culture that they can feel part of. All they have to do is first ask, then listen. This is where the kids growing up in this land will get their strength.

I think most Aboriginal people would agree with me that some structure is needed within the education system, not only with children, but with adults, where there is more hands-on teaching of Aboriginal culture by Aboriginal people. The more we are in a position to teach about ourselves, the stronger our people will grow and this will alleviate the loss of self-worth within a lot of Aboriginal people. Then we will begin to stop playing out that image projected onto us of being lazy and unable to work within the white structure of society.

If you tell anyone for long enough that they are hopeless, then they become hopeless. If you tell anyone for long enough that they have no culture, they will forget their culture. But as soon as the negatives are replaced with positives, and that person is told how good they are, the open wound begins to heal. That same person becomes positive, strong and confident of who they are. Then everyone around them benefits.

This change will happen with the teaching of our culture. That is where the strength lies to turn around the problems of lethargy, alcoholism, poor health, young people suiciding and us feeling lost within our own country.

My Aunty Val works a lot with young people in trouble. She says:

Our young people are full of anger. It comes out in different ways. Sometimes the aggression comes out on themselves – suicide – or on someone else – homicide or domestic violence. Glue sniffing is a type of suicide. The kids have been told it will kill them and they still do it because they want out. It's sad to see young ones that want out.

You have to heal their identity first. Their sense of identity is the most important thing to work on with these young ones. The whitefulla can't do that. You can't use the whiteman's ways. There are too many deep-down hurts in these kids. You have to go back to the old ways. When you know the tribal ways and you start using them with these kids, the ones petrol sniffing and trying to hurt themselves, it works, they respond.

Most of the time they're being what other people expect them to be. They're not being themselves.

You see, the whiteman is taught from a very young age that white is very special. White is pure and everything to do with white is good. Look at white people's storybooks. Everything good is white, like princesses, brides and angels. Everything evil is black, like witches and death. Now that has come down for generations.

What the Murris do now is take on that image, too. We start to think that because we are black we are bad. This is what is mixing these kids up. When I am working with these young ones who are in trouble, that's where I start. I start working on their sense of identity.

But, you see, the way things are structured at present is that there are industries within this country which are built on us staying down, out and dependent on hand-outs. This has been going on since Invasion Day. This is the way governments have kept us powerless. Just think how many non-Aboriginal people are employed to manage Aboriginal affairs and decide what is right for us. This is across the board, in areas of health, housing, justice, tourism, you name it. A good friend of mine once said, 'If all the blacks died tomorrow, then the next day there'd be a long line of white people queuing for the dole.' This man, Gary Foley, has a great gift of getting to the point.

My Uncle Peter Prior, Gullumbah, is my dad's eldest brother and the oldest member of the Birri-gubba clan. I used to stay with Uncle Peter and Aunty Milda all the time when I was a boy. They used to send me and my cousin Mervyn, who used to get me into trouble all the time, out hunting. I loved staying with them. Aunty Milda used to sweep the dirt floor and wipe it down. She would have that floor so shiny. Aunty used to cook up flying fox in this beautiful gravy and with those dough boys she makes.

Uncle Peter tells me lots of stories about our family on

Dad's side. This one story that he told me a while ago sticks in my mind in particular. He was on Palm Island in the days when you couldn't be black and you couldn't be white. He reckons you were just this thing in the middle with clothes on. But if visiting dignitaries came to the island, the overseers would get the Aboriginal people to discard their clothes, paint up, do some dances and sing their songs. My Uncle Peter described how he watched the visitors sipping their cups of tea and could see in their eyes the look of wonderment that who they saw as 'savages', dancing around 'primitively', had been 'tamed so effectively'. After the dignitaries left, it was back to the way things were – no singing of our songs, no speaking in our language, 'put your clothes on', 'learn to dance the foxtrot, the Pride of Erin', 'go to church on Sundays and sing hymns'.

My Uncle Peter says it was like being a performing animal in a circus. 'Okay, take your clothes off, put your monkey suit on and here's a banana.' Then after the performance they were told to get back out of their monkey suits, throw away the bananas and put their clothes back on. He says, 'In other words we were only black when they wanted us to be.'

Stories like this are common. We are starting to hear them because black people are now writing about themselves and what has really gone on in this country since the Invasion. I only recently became aware of why this story, among many others my uncle has told me, has stuck with me and frequently reappears in my mind. It's because nothing has changed. Though over fifty years have passed, the situation is still the same.

If the promotion of Aboriginal culture was as frantic in schools as it is within the tourist industry, Australian people would be more aware. But because there is no big financial gain to be made from Aboriginal culture in the education system, most Australians are left ignorant and their understanding of this country is stunted.

Tourism within Australia is one of the country's biggest industries. Tourism relies heavily on Aboriginal culture. Our knowledge of the past, our songs, dances and artwork are what the tourist industry needs for its trade. People come from all over the world for the purpose of experiencing the oldest continuous living culture in the world. They can see structures similar to the Opera House or the Sydney Harbour Bridge in their own countries. Next to the flora and fauna and the natural wonders of the land, we are what people come to see. And yet the attitude to us as people has not changed from those days on Palm Island that my Uncle Peter tells about.

The tourist industry wants our culture to make money but they don't want us. In other words, still, we are only black when they need us to be black. It hasn't altered how we are regarded. They need our culture for the economy of this country but they still don't respect us as people or treat us as equals.

Imagine how many non-Aboriginal people would be out of work if we were to close up shop and say we are not giving you any more. The tourist dollars stay in white hands. How much of the money that is earned by the selling of Aboriginal culture is going to the Aboriginal people whose culture it is? We still don't own what is ours.

There are many people working within the tourist industry who have great respect for Aboriginal culture and try their hardest to learn from and promote this culture with dignity. On the other hand, there are still too many that don't and who do not try to understand how complex the culture is that they're dealing with. Where I come from around Cairns, I know tourist operators who talk to visitors about the drunken blacks on the footpaths being hopeless and a disgrace. In the next breath, they'll be trying to sell the same tourists a boomerang or didjeridoo.

In one tourist brochure we are referred to as 'abos' and misinformation is given about the complexity of our language. At the same time, these tourist operators earn their living selling Aboriginal artefacts, telling the stories of the area and talking about bush medicine and food. Who did they get this from? The 'drunken blacks' that they talk about are the same people whose stories these are and whose paintings they sell.

A group of Aboriginal women artists were travelling over to Germany with their paintings and there was a big uproar in the paper back here because they got kicked out of this hotel and told they couldn't stay there because they were dirty. When the women came back, they were saying they didn't know what all the fuss was about. They get kicked out of places and told they can't stay in hotels all the time back here in their own country.

The way I feel, the position of Aboriginal people in the 1990s is like this. Imagine somebody walking into your house, pulling out a gun and shooting you half a dozen times, in your body, arms, legs, everywhere. Somehow you survive. The ambulance is called and you're whisked away to the hospital and you're put in intensive care with all these tubes coming out of your body, and the machine monitoring your heartbeat is going beep, beep, beep. The next day someone kicks the door open, walks in and says, 'Come on, I'm taking you for a run.' You can barely talk but you say, 'Can't you see I've been shot? I can't run.' Then the person says, 'Well, walk.' And you say, 'But I can't walk.' And the person says, 'You're okay. Come on.' And they drag you off the bed. You fall over but they still drag you. So, there you are, half crawling along the ground, half being dragged by the scruff of your neck. They pull out the tubes. The gaping holes made from all the bullets are weeping blood. There's blood all over the ground.

You see, that is like us now. We're still suffering from the first slaughter. We have gaping wounds that have never had a chance to heal. They only let us out of the concentration camps twenty-five years ago. We are still bleeding. Our blood is still pouring out, soaking the earth.

This image is always in the back of my mind. I had to go away from home to try and deal with it. Every Aboriginal person has to find their own way of dealing with this reality. If they can't deal with it they turn to alcohol or drugs, they get locked up, or they die.

You've got to remember that when white people think of Aboriginal people, they think of us as being drunk, lazy and all these negative stereotypes. That's all a lot of people see. But they forget we lived for fifty, sixty thousand years or more in a certain way and then, with the European Invasion, we were subjected to a hundred and eighty years of incarceration, being beaten, raped, poisoned, displaced, killed with disease and all these things. Suddenly, in the mid-sixties to seventies, the concentration camps were opened up. We were kicked out, and the government of the day says, 'Here's however many million dollars, go and change yourselves'. That's impossible. No race of people on earth could change and adopt a whole other lifestyle just with the click of a finger and some money.

Budda Paul used to say, 'You've got to try and play the whiteman's game and stay black while you're doing it.' Paul got confused because the whiteman's rules keep changing so many times. He did his best to fight the injustices of the white system, but it chewed him up and spat him out. That's what killed him.

The way I found to survive was through my time in the Air Force, then through music, my years behind the turn-tables DJing. Sport has been very important as well, particularly basketball. All the time, even when I was still up home, I was on the lookout for a structure to put myself in that would help me survive. Sport got me through a lot.

Succeeding at sport gave me a lot of confidence to take into other parts of my life. In the Rugby League competition in Townsville I played for Souths and won a premiership playing in the Under 16s. Even though Queensland is what you'd call a Rugby League state, I also won a premiership in Townsville with the Currajong Australian Rules Football Club. It felt good being top of the pile for once.

I kept playing competitive basketball through till I was twenty-five, that was in the Victorian Basketball Association, the strongest competition in Australia at that time. It was the forerunner to the National Basketball League. I coached the first Aboriginal women's team of any sport to tour outside Australia. In 1975 we had six basketball games in Aotearoa/New Zealand and we won three of them. In one exciting game we beat the top women's team in that country.

This year, Paul's son Jaii, who lives out at Alice Springs with his mother Maggie, phoned, wanting to come up home with me. I was rapt and I said to him, 'This will be good for you, my boy. You'll get to be amongst your cousins, and sit down and listen to your aunties and uncles. They've got a lot to teach you now.'

He's fifteen, you see, and should be learning the dances from his father's place. He said, 'Yeah, thanks, uncle, that's great. But I was hoping you could teach me about basketball.' I said, 'Eh, look out!' He jarred me up real good with that one, but I suppose it's fair enough, he needs to know about that, too.

Playing the game of basketball teaches you a lot about your strengths and weaknesses and how to make your weaknesses stronger and your strengths more powerful. If you are a scorer and you have a day where you can't buy a bucket, then you've got to help the team structure in other ways by tougher defence or trying to get more rebounds, blocking out on offensive and defensive boards, also supporting another person on the team who is scoring well so they can get clear. Going back to the basics is a good way to clear out any negative build-up within your own personal game. It stops you from becoming frustrated. It's the things that you do to yourself in your mind that let you and your team-mates down.

These lessons I learnt from sport are what have helped me survive a lot of challenges in other parts of my life. Both the mental and physical discipline go hand in hand. You learn about nutrition. Eating habits have to be watched so that you're fit to enjoy the game. Also remembering that there is a second half of your life which you want to enjoy as much as the first half.

I keep playing now whenever I can because, for me, basketball is a form of getting high. It's my relaxation. It helps me get away from the intensity of my work and what I face, say, at the schools or even when I was DJing. It gives you another option from going and getting bombed up on drugs or alcohol.

When you go down to the courts to play, you aren't an Aboriginal, you aren't a blackfulla, you are just somebody who plays within the structure of a team and can shoot and screen. You yell and scream, swear, push and shove and it's good fun. You hook up with a team and those team-mates rely on you to win the game so you can play the next game.

When you walk onto the court, you leave behind all that you do everywhere else. It doesn't matter who you are before that moment. You go out and there are a lot of physical things to concentrate on and they take your mind away from the pressures in the rest of your life.

Sport takes you into another world where all you are is just another fulla who plays basketball. Unlike in my teenage years when we played sport in situations where there wasn't the mix of cultures, down the basketball court there's whitefullas, blackfullas, Asian fullas, all kinds of fullas. Nobody is anybody but a basketball player. It's not a matter of colour. It's just whether this person has the physical and mental abilities to beat you.

Just that sensation of running up and down the court is great. It relieves a lot of stress, though sometimes my godson Ciaran chastises me for swearing too much. 'Mont, Mont,' he says, and he points his finger at me while I'm still on the court. After the game he says, 'You don't need to say those things.' He gives me a slap on the hand for each swear word I've said. Of course he's right. Ten-year-olds are never wrong!

You sit down after the game with the boys and talk about anything and everything. Some people I've played with for ten years and suddenly you find out where they come from. Because when you go down to the courts it's just 'how you going, mate', 'how you been', and it's just wonderful.

You have to do more preparation as you get older. Yoga is very important to keep your flexibility. Also, the fact that you still contribute within the team structure feels good. I played in the World Masters Games in Brisbane in 1994. We won silver; the Americans beat us. But we got to the grand final. Also our Myths and Legends team won gold and silver in the Australian Championships over the past few years. We talk about the times we played against each other and the scores are always higher and the shots get further and further away from the basket every year.

What I do in schools is very competitive, too, just within a different structure. The two worlds meet when I have a shoot around with the kids during lunchbreaks. Usually the basketball court is in the gym where I perform. Before each performance I try to do a stretching and warm-up exercise routine, especially in winter. If I can get my hands on a basketball I shoot around till the kids come in. There I am, in my little red judda jah, paint all over me, standing outside the three-point line shooting. The kids often can't believe I can shoot a basketball. Sometimes neither can I. I remember one boy saying, 'Wow! Did Aboriginal people invent basketball, too?' I said to him, 'No, no, it was Doctor Naismith.' He probably thought Naismith was a witchdoctor from a Northern Territory mob.

I look forward to the weekends, like most people. But to me, the weekends are very important because that's my time off. I need to take a break from talking about black issues. In some cases, when I address secondary schools, I'm the whipping boy and they vent all their anger on me. I'm visible and a target for the relief of their frustrations and misconceptions. I'm in the firing line every day. I'll never stop being proud of my blackness but you need to take time off to breathe. It's like running a marathon every day of the week and then running a marathon all weekend. You need a break. Immersing myself in a sport that I love clears my mind and by Monday I'm ready to face the issues of being black again.

I can remember Paul telling me that he had this fight one time and it was over our sister Kimmy and it was with this big migaloo fulla, big whitefulla. Paul said this big fulla hit him a couple of times, hit him real hard and his legs started to go. He just shook his head, 'I can't fall down. I can't fall down.' He just shook his head and kept saying, 'I can't fall down' until he beat the big whitefulla.

When you're in my situation, it's more psychological and it's more in the heart that you have to take these beatings. There's many times that I've felt like falling over but you know you can't fall over because you might die.

I know that sounds drastic and dramatic, but there is so much pressure on you. Which means that it goes back to all the other things I say about avoidance of alcohol and drugs to make you strong to face up to the pressure. Some weeks it's like you do a grand final in each show and then you travel one hundred kilometres the next day to another grand final.

If I fell down, I'd be letting my mum and dad down, I'd be letting down my two brothers, my sister and my nephew who died, and I'd be letting down my uncles and aunties who have suffered for years as well. You can't let them down.

Because being a communicator is my strength, it's really important that I keep level. You try and make the down periods less and the up periods more. That's why it comes back to being aware of your body and being healthy, then, when the down periods come, you can deal with them. Doing yoga and meditation and these things are very important to the way you cope.

As a blackfulla, you can't fall down. You fall down, you die.

For a long while I didn't know why I went off to the city and did all these things: football, basketball, modelling, DJing . . . Now I know why.

It was all to do with me being a link, one of the many links. There are a lot of people who are links across this land. The links between Aboriginal culture and the white people.

5

FINDING MY WAY
BACK HOME

All I need is to hear their voices.

I never turned my back on this place, Yarrabah, even though I grew up in Townsville and then moved away down south. It's the strength I get from Yarrabah that makes me able to get up and communicate with audiences of white people. You can't explain it. Your spirit is here. It is a feeling all around you. A track of black mothers through time immemorial. There's nothing to beat that.

When my nieces and nephews look up at me I remember how I was. When you see your cousins, your blood relations, those who cry for you, you know you are not alone. Yarrabah has always been my strength. It is where my mother's people are from.

Whenever I go back to Yarrabah, one of my aunties, Aunty Pauline, makes a big fuss. She cries and runs to me, hugs and kisses me and says, 'Oh, my boy, where you bin?'

She always gives me whatever she's got – fish or turtle, dugong, crab – to take back for Mum and Dad. Aunty knows all the stories of this place. It is hard for her, I see that in her eyes. She sees all our people drowning in the poisons supplied by the whites. She is often drowning herself. Often she wants to forget what has happened.

The title 'Maybe Tomorrow' comes from what Aunty Pauline said to me one day when I was sitting having a cup of tea at Cousin Bobby's place and talking about writing this book. As we were talking, Aunty was clapping and singing traditional songs, stamping her feet into the lino. When she finished she caught her breath and said, 'You know, I can tell you fullas lotta deadly stories. I can sing you lotta deadly songs and do lotta deadly dancin'. I could write you a deadly book too.' She stopped, waved her arms in the air and shrugged her shoulders, then said, 'Nah! Maybe tomorrow. Maybe tomorrow.' I gave her a hug and said, 'Whenever you want. Thank you, my beautiful aunty.'

My great-great-grandmother on my mother's side is Mandal Kala. Yarrabah and Kiriga (Cape Grafton), and Mira Warikal (King Beach) – the place of the Medicine Water, the Sacred Waterhole, Bana Yelimaka – is her tribal land, the land of the Kunggandji people. Great-great-nanna Mandal Kala's daughter, Kerata – Granny Jinnah Katchwan – was the first of our people to be brought down from the hills to the mission at Yarrabah. My great-great-nanna Mandal Kala, was killed by a neighbouring tribe and Granny Jinnah was left wounded by a club. She was only a little girl. The missionaries who found her nursed her to health. So then Granny Jinnah grew up on the Yarrabah mission.

Father John Gribble, an Anglican priest, set up Yarrabah in 1892 as an Anglican mission. He saw that Aboriginal people were dying as the white people took more and more land. He wanted to create somewhere where Aboriginal people would be saved from this destruction. Lots of white people at the time didn't want an Aboriginal reserve near Cairns but eventually it went ahead. John Gribble gave all his life's savings to set up Yarrabah.

When the mission was opened, Murris were suspicious and reluctant to leave the safety of the mountains. Later on, when the government took over Yarrabah, it became a very different place from Gribble's original dream of 'Utopia'. Aboriginal ways were forbidden then, and a lot of half-caste children stolen from their parents were sent to grow up in the dormitories there to learn the white ways.

My grandfather Eugene Stell and his sister Nanna Rosie were taken away from their parents and brought to Yarrabah. Nanna Susie, my grandmother and Granny Jinnah Katchwan's daughter, was taken off Granny Jinnah and put in the dormitory at Yarrabah. Her father was a whiteman, Bert Gribble, son of Father John Gribble. It caused a real scandal at the time. Granny Jinnah was only fifteen and he would only have been young, too. He was sent away from Yarrabah and none of our family heard of him again.

121

Their daughter, Nanna Susie, was taken away from her family and, like all Aboriginal people on reserves at the time, was forbidden to speak her language or learn about her culture. She grew up in the dormitory on Yarrabah.

My Uncle Henry Fourmile grew up on Yarrabah and was taken from his family, too, and put in the dormitory. He describes how it was:

When we were ten years old we were forced to go to the dormitory to live till we were sixteen. It was like a prison. We were let out a full day on Saturday and a half day on Sunday. Any other day you could only see your family through the fence. That's how we lost our culture. They tried to stop our language. Most of my people, the Yidinji, stayed all together, away from the main mission and we could keep our culture going more that way.

At the dormitory, we had one blanket for the floor to sleep on and one to cover you. We'd be woken at six in the morning to go down to church, come back, have breakfast then go to school. After school we'd just stay in the dorm. It was a hard life.

My family were still maintaining their culture living off the land. I was with my father all the time before I was taken off to the dormitory.

But the old people had ways and means of passing things on so the culture stayed alive, and they had ways and means of protecting themselves. My Aunty Val, Nanna Susie's daughter and my mother's sister, says their mum told them over and over again not to look into white people's eyes. 'Whenever you look at the white-man, don't look into their eyes. You look between their eyes, at their forehead, but never in their eyes. If you look into their eyes they can pass their evil on to you.'

When my mother was thirteen she met her Granny Jinnah. She couldn't talk to her because of the language barrier. Mum describes how they both got so frustrated trying to communicate. But she told me how Granny Jinnah welcomed her with open arms. She said, 'I knew how much my grandmother had suffered and that she loved her daughter Susie and us. I felt so proud.'

My grandmother Susie married my grandad Eugene Stell on Yarrabah. The authorities accused Grandad Eugene of inciting a riot and getting people to strike on the reserve. As punishment, he and his family were sent to Palm Island in 1916. He died when I was a baby.

Palm Island was a penal settlement. Islanders, Maoris, Aboriginals, all kinds of people were sent there. Anyone who was thought to be a troublemaker was sent to Palm. That's how it was set up. It was government-run, but the churches, the Baptist, Anglican and Catholic churches, had a big influence on the lives of Aboriginal people held there. When half-caste children were taken away from their families in other parts of Queensland, they would be sent to Yarrabah and when it was overcrowded they were sent to Palm.

My grandfather on my father's side was from the Birri-gubba Nations, whose homelands constituted the Bowen Basin area and extended up as far as the Ross River in Townsville. His people were removed from that area and taken to Palm Island to make way for pastoralists and land grabbers. Dad's mother, my grandmother, was Kanak. At the turn of the century, South Sea Islander people were stolen from their homelands and brought across to Australia, in particular Queensland, to work in the cane fields as slave labour. They became known as Kanaks. My father was born on Palm Island.

Being on the reserves meant you had to watch your culture and your people die slowly. Being off the reserves meant you could be shot and killed outright. On the reserves you were taught to be third-, fourth-, fifth-, sixth-best. You used to have to walk several paces behind white people and pick up what they dropped.

That's what Dad got into trouble for. At fifteen he refused to call a white boy of a similar age 'sir'. The Palm Island authorities, who were white, got the native police involved. They gave my dad one hell of a beating. Then my Uncle Peter and a friend went after the four native police. My Uncle Peter tells me that day there was blood and bones flying everywhere.

After that the superintendent dumped my dad in a boat and got him shipped off to the mainland, Lucinda Point near Ingham. An Italian farmer took him in and Dad started working for him cutting cane. My father tells me that this man really took care of him and eventually became Dad's godfather. After that, Dad worked on cattle stations, in the shearing sheds, all over the place, before he and Mum married and moved to Townsville.

Mum described to me a very significant occasion that drew together a few of these threads from the past. Recently, a celebration was held by the Anglican church to commemorate one hundred years since Yarrabah Mission was established. Mum says:

Two of my sisters, Norma and Val, and I went up to Cairns especially for that day. It was a really beautiful celebration. They had a big sit-down feast with dancing. Everyone was invited. There were hundreds of people. One of the descendants of the original Father John Gribble was there. He was a priest from Rockhampton.

My sister Val was determined to tell the Gribbles that we were related. She kept nudging me and saying, 'I'm going to tell him about what happened.' I felt very embarrassed and felt the timing was wrong. 'You don't just plonk things like that in people's laps.' But she kept on and on and, eventually, went up and said to him, 'We are related.'

We got a very different reaction from what we expected. We expected that they might be embarrassed or reject us or just be very polite. He said he believed what my sister was saying. Then he left us for a moment and went off and spoke to three women who were part of the Gribble family.

They all came back over to join us. Each of them wanted to sit down and talk. They really were thrilled to meet us and made everyone feel at ease. They took photos of our whole family group together and wanted to know more about us. It was great that they felt so happy about meeting relations they never knew they had. They were members of a religious order too, Christian people, and they opened their hearts to us.

We've been writing and exchanging bits of the past ever since, photos of our grandparents and great-grandparents and so on. One of the Gribble women, Lorna, invited all of us up to meet again a year or so later when she was passing through Cairns. She wanted to know the family tree from our side. She said it was quite fashionable now to have Aboriginal relatives and she was pleased to have us as relations. Later, she sent me a photo of Bert Gribble.

I am fortunate that I can trace my ancestry back to my Dreaming place. I feel sorry for those of my people who have no way of tracing their family. The connection with the Gribbles is like finding the missing link of my white ancestry. I haven't met Lorna, the Gribble relation my mum is now in contact with, but I have read her letters. Looking at this photo she sent to my mum of my great-grandfather, a whiteman whose family was from Cornwall, I had mixed feelings. Not knowing the circumstances of their relationship, it's hard for me to have an opinion one way or the other about the man I saw looking out at me from this photo, my great-grandfather. We have always known our black ancestry. Now this connection has been made we can trace our white ancestors and by doing this it fills in the missing pieces to the puzzle.

The struggle to survive on and off reserves like Yarrabah and Palm Island still goes on. You have all this pain as well as this beauty. It is this combination of extremes that can still leave you very confused.

It's dangerous there – the disruption, the alcoholism, all the pain . . . My cousin Paul Fourmile, who lives on Yarrabah, says, 'I'm happy when my people die. They have no more pain. They rest in peace then. Us that are still alive, we got that pain of fighting for our survival all the time.' But at the same time it's a safe place. It's the birthplace of my people. It's the land. It's the people. The people are the land.

You're a bit scared when you are away for so long. Sometimes, within yourself, you feel like an outcast because you are forced to leave, to alienate yourself, to survive. But if you haven't given in or sold out then you know within yourself that you always belong here.

When I'm way down south, I sometimes think I'm all alone fighting these battles, but then I remember that I've got this huge family that I belong to. My mother seems to know when I'm in trouble. Sometimes, I'll be in a state of depression and the phone rings and it's her. Just one word, two words, from my mum and dad and I'm strong. All I need is to hear their voices. It's like putting a shell to your ear and hearing the sea crashing. When I hear my mother's voice, I know I have this ocean of strength from a whole group of people that goes back for all that long time. I don't take it for granted. I might not always feel how strong it is but through my people I know it is there.

When I go back up home, the old people say, 'Where you bin? You better come back. Us old fullas gonna go soon and you need to come back and learn it all.' They say, 'You bin away long enough. You come back and learn here.'

Some of the stories that I'm telling now in schools, I've only just heard over the last five to ten years. Like the one I tell about the crocodile is from Old Man Esau Miller. When he told me that one, it felt like that story had always been with me. It's like you belong to that story. Even when I tell about the hill up at Yarrabah and the old man looking for the water, I feel like I've known that for a long time. I think that feeling of belonging allows you to tell these stories.

I have to spend time with all my uncles and aunties. They have got a lot to teach me now. It's time for me to do this because I'm starting to be an elder. It's important to do this. That is what Mum and Dad fought for, to keep the culture, that's what everyone else fought for. Not for me to just go and get lost in the city and forget about it.

To go back and learn these things is really important.

There are certain things that you learn off your aunties and certain things that you learn off your uncles and then other things that you learn off your mother and father. In my understanding, this is to keep the family structure, you are connected to everyone. You go to each aunty or each uncle for certain information. Your cousins are very important too and you can learn a lot off them, like I learn from my cousin Gerry Fourmile.

Blackfullas can tell some really good stories. Storytelling is a part of us. My cousins can sit down and tell stories that will make you hurt yourself from laughing too much. When we get together, us blackfullas, we laugh all the time. At home you are around your cousins and you muck around telling jokes, talking stupid, yakkaiing, which is screaming out and poking each other. We laugh at situations, we laugh at ourselves, even at the saddest times. Like when my sister Kimmy died, when she hanged herself.

I got on a plane and went straight up home. My niece Cherie was with me. When they found Kimmy she was still alive. I was hoping she would hold on till I got there. I wanted to kiss her and tell her how much I loved her. She was in the hospital and when the plane stopped in Sydney and then in Brisbane I kept phoning up. My mum told her I was coming, and they could see she knew. But she died before I could get there. She died when I was at the Brisbane airport.

The next day we went to the morgue where we could view her body. I touched her face and it was like ice. I

129

kissed her and told her I loved her. I went back out with the others. We were sitting outside on the side of this flowerbed that was like a seat. A lot of our family was there. We were all grieving that much for her.

My nephew Kawangi, he is an amazing boy. He has been blind since birth and he has a special way of knowing when to say things. He said, 'Uncle Monty, this is a really sad time, isn't it?' I said, 'Yes, Kawangi, she was very beautiful, your Aunty Kimmy.' We were all sitting around crying and trying to cope with our loss. I will always remember looking at the face of Kimmy's son Bidju coming out from being with his mum for the last time.

After a while longer, Kawangi says, 'Uncle Monty, what's that thing Aunty Kimmy's in? What do you call that thing, that box?' 'It's called a coffin, Kawangi.' It was really quiet. Then through the quiet I could hear this little cough, 'hu, hu'. Kawangi was coughin'. He made us all laugh. He knew we needed it. He wanted to break the mood, change the direction, even if it was only for a brief moment's relief. He gave us a way we could laugh even in our deepest sorrow, and we felt stronger. It helped us go back into that grief and be closer to her the way she knew us.

You see, that's the way we survive. That humour gets us through. Being stupid and yakkaiing even in the worst times. When you get back down south in the big city, you can see migaloo people thinking, 'We don't poke here and we don't yakkai, whatever that word is.' I'm different down there. I'm still me, but I know I change the way I talk.

One time I rang up my beautiful sister Chicky, she's my craziest sister. I rang her up for a chat and after a while she said, 'Aaaaa, you sound like a whitefulla, you.' And I said, 'Eh, look out!', and she said, 'That's better.' It's not a conscious thing but down south you have to be really tense and alert. When you get home you can just relax. After that, I used to ring Chicky up and joke and say, 'There's this whitefulla looking for you again. This white boy wants to speak to his sister!'

Trying to keep your blackness while working within the white society, you end up copping flak from both sides. Blackfullas on one side hang it on you because they think you are on the other side trying to be white. Actually, it's within the structure of yourself as to whether you are changeable or not. Everyone changes in life. But like I've said before, I never in my heart really left home. Even though there were chances in holidays to go overseas, come Christmas and Easter I would always go home.

You still have to prove yourself. Within your group, Aboriginal people are very conscious that you don't become up yourself. If that happens and you come home with airs and graces, then your family will all line up and flog you. And so you say, 'Well, I'll bring me back down to earth.' That's why I've still got a rust bucket of a car. I love it. I feel comfortable in Rusty. The way I feel is that if I got a flash new car and I'm driving around and none of my family have one, I don't really feel like I deserve it. You know what I mean?

131

Even when I first started writing this book, I was a bit apprehensive because I was tied up in the individuality of myself. Blackfullas can't be too deadly. You can't shine out above anyone else in your own family. Then when Meme gave me the first draft, we were sitting down having a pizza in Bondi. After I read it through, I looked up and all I could see was my mother standing beside my sister Kimmy's grave and she was sobbing. That's all I could see. Then I realised this book is really for her because she never cried for Paul or Nick. She had to be really strong. With Kimmy she just sobbed. She couldn't bear the pain any more. All black mothers, like my mother, have to bear so much.

The concern I had with my individuality just went straight out the window then. I feel like I am the vehicle and my family are all the spirits that drive that vehicle. Individuality, that isn't important.

Anybody who is lost or separated from their family wants to find out their background. That's where their strength lies. Even till the day they die every possible effort is made to find their way back so they can die in peace. It's the same with Aboriginal people. Everybody needs that strength. The strength of knowing who you are, where you come from and what you believe. I think you need the ability to find your inner strength from the strength that has come from a long time ago, from the ancestors.

My nephew Karl
Fourmile, language
name Mar-roon
*When I put it on (this
ochre that comes from
the earth), nothing can
touch me. It's my shield
or my plate of armour.*

My nephew Greg Fourmile, language name Wuwan
What reconciliation has to achieve is a state of mutual respect.

My nephew Kawangi
Pryor
*He has been blind since
birth and he has a
special way of knowing
when to say things.*

My nieces Paulani
Winitana, Dawn Smith
and Shandelle Prior
*We know we all belong to
each other and that is our
strength, you see.*

My nephews Leon and Kenny Ray Pryor and, in the middle,
my niece Viella Pryor

*They (white people) see us living in the white way and often
they don't realise that we are still living by the beliefs and ways
of our ancestors.*

My nephew Kurtis Pryor

*I say they go to three schools ... the third school is learning how
to protect yourself from the authorities.*

My nephew Sean Pryor
'I hope they don't take anyone else because I only had a little heart and now there's no more left.'

My nephew Nicky Bidju Pryor
I will always remember looking at the face of Kimmy's son Bidju coming out from being with his mum for the last time.

My niece Njrami Fourmile

It's very important for young Aboriginal people to wake up and say, 'I am black', and to feel strong about their Aboriginality. This gives them the strength to deal with their early teens.

My nephews Ngarrayi Maree and Valdis Valodze, language name Gaban, and my niece Dzinta Valodze, language name Janal

When my nieces and nephews look up at me I remember how I was.

My nieces Ginny Katchwan Patterson and Esmay Dolly Patterson
Children in Aboriginal culture don't have a say as such, but they have a role to play, as does everyone within the group.

My nieces Mandal Kala and Nunjil Pryor and, in the middle, Meme's daughter Grace Cockatoo Lovell
If people can see the beauty of Aboriginal culture, which is this country, then this will be a much happier place.

My godson Ciaran Ward and me
I get my strength to stay focused from my mum and dad and from my beautiful godson Ciaran.

My nephew Bernard Riley
at eighteen months old
*Children always seem to
bridge the gap. Like music,
if you listen to them and
follow their lead, your spirit
will dance.*

I organised to have this photograph of my family taken just
before I left for the Air Force in 1968

TOP ROW, LEFT TO RIGHT:
My brother Nick, me, my father, my mother, my sisters Sue,
Chrissy and Cilla

BOTTOM ROW, LEFT TO RIGHT:
My brothers Roscoe and Paul, my sisters Kim, Chicky, Chubby
and Toni.

Once you find that, that's a lot of strength. And that makes you more powerful as a person.

It's very important for young Aboriginal people to wake up and say, 'I am black', and to feel strong about their Aboriginality. This gives them the strength to deal with their early teens. When you don't have enough faith within yourself, that's when you are vulnerable. You take alcohol or drugs or get into trouble because of this.

You have more of a chance to survive if you pride yourself on who you are. The system is very well versed in taking this pride away from Aboriginal people. Not only physically taking it away, like taking away children, but mentally and spiritually by still trying to destroy those links with your culture. Like my mother says, 'Our people are dying because they have no pride. Their pride has been kicked out of them.'

It's the same with these kids that are locked up. I went out to Girrakool Detention Centre in Kariong near Gosford. It's the maximum security centre for young boys who've done pretty tough offences. There were one or two Italian boys and a few other whitefullas but the overwhelming majority of the boys are blackfullas.

When I spoke to them it was like I was with my own family. I included everyone that was present at the workshop. I told them that the spirit that is angry and the spirit that hurts itself is the one that's lost. They are probably in this situation from being lost.

I tell them, 'Don't walk behind anyone. Allow yourself to be angry. By doing this, the anger is not bottled

133

up and it doesn't become a time bomb. That anger is defused when you go back to find your roots. Then you are able to grow from that.'

I also spoke to them about my brothers Nick and Paul, and my sister Kim. They understood because they knew I wasn't a social worker, counsellor or with a government department on a mission to save their wretched black souls. They could see I was being straight with them and spoke from the heart. They must have, because they got up to do the dances. We sat down and talked afterwards and they said, 'Look, brother, how do we find out about where we come from?' I spoke to them about the different organisations in the Sydney area that they could contact to help them find their way.

I said, 'We need Aboriginal people, like you, to be the teachers.' I looked across and saw the look in their faces when I said, 'You're really needed and you're wanted. There's not many of us. We need us to learn more about ourselves. Because that is important for the strength of this whole country. So, your strength is needed. You have to be strong now so that when your time is up and you get out, you don't do a U-turn and return to the same place.'

After, we just sat down and talked and I told them a few jokes and stories about my life. They couldn't believe that you could make a living off being black – from teaching about your culture, like stories, songs, dances, foods, medicine . . . there is so much we have to teach. They all broke up laughing when I told them that there are a lot of white people out there teaching about us and getting paid for it.

In suggesting to them that they get out there and start communicating to whitefullas, I'm not saying, 'Okay, get a big peace sign round your neck and carry flowers and say, "Peace brother"'. I'm just saying, 'Well, this is how I've survived this far. What works for me may not work for you. But then again, it might.' I take some aspects of what I use to survive and explain it to them. I'm not a great one for drinking and I don't do drugs. What I worked out long ago was drink when you're happy, don't drink when you're sad. Whatever you like to do, don't do it when you're depressed 'cos you get more depressed and that's when the hurt and pain comes in. I tell them if you want to do these things then you do them but if you avoid those pitfalls it makes your path in life less dangerous. Avoidance of the pitfalls is important.

I am always aware that it could be me sitting in those cells.

I talk a lot about my brother when I'm with these boys. I saw what the system did to him. He'd been in jail, locked up and beaten up even before he was a teenager. As an Aboriginal kid, when we were young, you expected to get into trouble with the bullymen. For them to beat you when they locked you up was normal. It hasn't changed for generations, this. What Paul went through is the same as what our parents and grand-parents had to face. And still my nieces and nephews are facing the same treatment. Nothing has changed.

I can remember my mother telling me this story. She and Dad had only been married a couple of years. She got a phone call saying Dad was down the lockup. She grabbed some money for bail and jumped on her bike and headed off to the police station. She passed this man staggering up the road. She didn't know him so she went on past. She heard the Pryor whistle – we've got this whistle that our whole family recognise – and she realised it was her husband. She couldn't recognise him because the coppers had beaten him so bad. His face was all busted up. She helped him home and patched him up.

Before Paul committed suicide at my house in Melbourne, he was in trouble at Yarrabah. The police called him a troublemaker because he stood up for his rights. He was black and strong, the same as his grandfather and father. When they were too strong, they were labelled troublemakers and shifted to another reserve. The same with Paul. The coppers wanted to shift him off Yarrabah, too, but with the different laws of the day, they had to do it a different way. So, as they do now, the police provoked Paul to react so they could take him in to the lockup, handcuff him and beat him. He was a repeat offender, you see. His grandfather was black, his father was black and he was black. They almost killed him.

After he went to the hospital and got photos taken, Paul charged the police with assault. They, in turn, charged him with assaulting a police officer. My family and friends went to the court to support him. After a while the police came out and said there was a delay, so the family could go off and get a cup of tea, which they did. While they were away, the police took Paul into the children's court – he was twenty-eight – locked the doors and tried him there. He was all alone. He was charged with assaulting a police officer, and was sentenced to three months community service.

He tried to do his time, but the police kept harassing him, saying things like, 'We'll finish you off next time.' His idea was it was better to be on the run and alive than at home and dead so he skipped the rest of his punishment up there and came to Melbourne to stay with me. He lived in terror of being sent back to Yarrabah to finish his time up there. Within a few months, after a series of incidents with the Melbourne police, he landed in the Fitzroy lockup.

By the time he was released from there he was a mess. He could take beatings, he could take a gun being stuck to his head, but who can take their own shit being rubbed in their face? The humiliation of it was too much. I looked into his eyes and I could see that he was dead. I sat with him and tried to talk but he threw his arms up and walked away. He said he was all right but I knew he wasn't.

I was still DJing at the time. It was a Saturday night. I came home around four on the Sunday morning to find all the doors open. I found his clap sticks on the front step. I thought he must have gone away for a while so I went about my business as usual. It wasn't until the Wednesday that I walked down to the back shed to get something and I noticed this foul smell. I looked over to the left and saw my brother's crumpled body lying on the floor of the shed all puffed and swollen. He had a piece of rope around his neck and there was blood all over the floor. He'd climbed up on the bench and jumped off. The rope had snapped his neck at the same time as it broke. His body was covered in ochre, painted up for corroboree.

Our family brought pressure to bear so that Paul's death was investigated under the Royal Commission into Aboriginal Deaths in Custody. In July 1990, Commissioner Wootten, QC concluded his preliminary report by saying, '. . . the Tribunal was also of the view that, if Mr Pryor was alive, it would have no hesitation in recommending criminal charges against them [the police officers from Yarrabah].' Instead of the police officers being brought to justice, the report simply concluded that their 'conduct fell below the standard expected of a police officer' and that they both 'should be reminded of his [their] obligation to strictly comply with General Instruction 7.42, as required by Rule 50 of the Police Rules 1978'.

My sister Chicky still has to teach her kids how to protect themselves from the bullymen. She says:

All through the thirteen years of my oldest son, Liam's, life, I kept pushing it into him. 'You don't answer back. You just give the coppers your name and address and you just walk away.' Our kids have to learn this. Even if they pull you up ten times a day and ask the same questions. We have to teach our kids to walk away and not react to the abuse they get. We haven't got the system in place to defend ourselves otherwise.

One night Liam came home and said, 'They only pulled us over for our bikes, no light on our bikes, so I said, "You know where I live." They said, "Yes, Tamarind Street, Liam Pryor. You're a very popular little man aren't you, Liam?" So, next time, Mum, I'm going to put a light on my bike and get myself a helmet and even have receipts for everything to prove I don't steal. One less thing they can pull us up for.'

Liam had no respect for the coppers when he heard what they did to his Uncle Paulie on Yarrabah. He saw the photographs of him taken after he was beaten. Liam could feel for Paulie. He hated the coppers because of that. What we pump into our children every day is what happened to their Uncle Nicky and Uncle Paul. They are only young kids, not even teenagers. They shouldn't have to know these things.

Liam was branded by the coppers. They wouldn't leave him alone. They hassle all the Murri kids. They frisk them, they name call, 'nigger', 'boong', and all the rest, threaten them, putting their gloves on and saying they'll take them for a trip down the station. This really puts the wind up the kids.

Liam was a passenger in a stolen car. The car he was in crashed into a tree. They were being chased by the police. They reckon the car my boy was in was travelling at 130 km/h when it crashed. Two other young boys were in the car. They survived. My darling boy died at 5.22 in the morning. The coppers didn't come round till 11.30 that morning.

I would have been more gentle on him if I had known. The last two weeks with him were beautiful. We had a beautiful time in those two weeks like somehow we were given that special time. I gave him a bit of slack. I let him stay up a bit late, and sleep in my bed some nights. Liam, my boy, he was so heartful. He used to bring home streeties and ask if we could share our dinner with them because their mum had turfed them out of home. He was showing me how skinny this one kid was, saying, 'Look, Mum, he hasn't had a feed for decades!' His little mate wasn't even ten years old. Liam would sleep on the floor and give them his bed.

I couldn't even walk when I had to go up to the morgue. I kept hoping they had made a mistake. My mum was with me. I wanted her there. When I finally looked at him, his body was all screwed up with just one eye open staring at me. 'Mum, it's true, it's him, there's no mistake.' I just threw myself over him.

When I came out, his little brother Seany kept asking, 'Was it him, was it him?' 'Yes, my darling, it's your brother.' He fainted. Then he wanted to go in and see him. 'Can't we take him home just for one more night to be all together? Why can't we take him home? I want to give him a bogey – a bath – and warm him up. Stupid migaloo people's laws, why can't we take him home?'

Mum came down with me. I felt for my mum. I said, 'You already been through this three times.' I just looked at her and wondered how she copes. Three times she has been to the morgue to see her dead children.

I didn't care how cold he was, I just lay beside him. They tried to drag me away but I swore and fought them. No bastard is going to tell me to stop crying. Losing your child is like your last bit of breast milk being drained from you, and there is no more life left in your body. I would never wish that even on my worst enemy.

Long before the whiteman came, we were passing on stories and legends. We are still doing that today, only the stories are of sorrow and loss. My grandmothers have had to pass on the vision of their children dying and the

141

pain that goes with that. I watch my mother as she continues this tradition and I cry.

My mum says:

When they brought Nicky's body home, it was in the back of the ute, and I went over and I could feel all my strength go and I was going to collapse or something. But then I remember just switching into this other state. And I knew I couldn't, I had to organise things. Contact the ambulance, phone the police. I phoned Father Pat Mullins then. I would have to wait till tomorrow to cry.

The ambulance men worked on him for a length of time trying to revive him but eventually I had to accept that he was gone. When you think of them gone, and how they've gone, the pain you feel inside takes over. That pain won't go away. The tears may have dried, but you never stop grieving.

Nine months after my nephew died, a court case was held and the other two boys in the car with Liam were brought up on charges. This was a very hard time for my sister Chicky. She and other members of my family sat in the court and, as usual, had to listen to the police and the lawyers describe Liam like he was a criminal and this was all his fault. I said to my sister, 'Don't you give a stuff about what anybody says about your boy, it's what you know about him that counts. You knew him and what he was like. That's the image that we all have to keep in our minds. Not the tainted image that was created in the courtroom. In the end, what we know about our boy is all that matters.'

Chicky keeps saying that all she wants to know is the truth of what happened the night Liam died. Did the police car bump them off the road, as one witness, who later refused to make a written statement, told her? She wants to know the truth so she can tell his two brothers and they can go on from there. Now she has to handle trying to keep these two young boys alive and stay alive herself.

The other day the coppers pulled Sean and Kurtis over and said, 'I hope you Pryor boys have learnt your lesson. Your big brother's dead now.' Seany came in crying. He's only nine. He's got so much hate for them. He told me, 'When I grow up, Mum, I want to be a bully-man but I'll be putting all of them away.'

They want to wag school when the coppers come to give a lecture. I try to tell them just to sit there. Maybe think of something they would like to ask them. Seany says, 'All I want to ask them is why they took my brother.'

In the court, one of the boys who survived the crash said that as Liam was dying his last words were, 'If I don't make it, tell my mum I love her.'

His little brother, Sean, was crying with his mum the other day. He said:

When we lost Uncle Nicky a chunk was taken out of my heart. When we lost Uncle Paulie, another chunk of my heart was taken. Then when we lost

Aunty Kimmy, another chunk of my heart was gone. But, Mum, when they took my brother, they took the rest. I hope they don't take anyone else because I only had a little heart and now there's no more left.

As a family we try to deal with these tragedies. After Kimmy's death, I remember sitting down around the tree in the front yard of Mum and Dad's house. Our family was having a talk about why it happened and what we've got to do to stop any more deaths like this in our family. Jason, my nephew, who was sixteen then, was getting angry and sounding off about how he would react if the coppers pulled him up. 'You don't do that,' one of my sisters said, 'I don't want to see you hanging off a tree, too.' But Jason's anger and confusion has to be addressed in a way that will help him to understand how to cope if a situation like that occurs. For this to happen, straightforward answers must be given.

Lakaya, Paul's daughter, asked her mother Juliet why her Aunty Kim had committed suicide. She kept asking, 'Why does this keep happening? Why are people dying like this all the time? If my dad was so strong, why did he kill himself?' Juliet couldn't give her a clear answer because she was still searching for these answers herself.

Having to deal with these tragedies, plus the misinterpretation from the police, on top of everything else like rubbish in the media that helps form racist community attitudes, it gets like being in a cesspool, a whirlpool.

You've got to get out of there, you've got to climb out and rest, wash off and have a sleep. Then you come back and dive right back in. But these fullas, my brothers, my sister and my nephew, they never got a chance to get out.

It got very hard for my brothers and sister not to see any progress or light. I think that comes from being in a one-dimensional place where there is not much chance to develop your mind. Their spirituality was being stifled. Take, for example, this one article I have here that was in the Cairns newspaper recently. It talks about Daniel Yock, the young Aboriginal dancer who died while in custody. The journalist makes fun of his death in this article. 'Yack-ity, Yackity, Yock' was the headline they used. He went on to say we should take our medicine and stop whingeing about it. Multiply this one article X amount of times over X amount of years, imagine that? If you add to that the other two main forms of media, television and radio, then that's a pretty intense whirlpool of negativity to survive in.

When you look at this same situation happening in Aboriginal families across the country, you realise that you are part of a much bigger cycle of tragedy. This cycle has been going on since Invasion Day. Our children today are aware of the problems their ancestors have had with the white law. Generations down the track the bullymen are still repeating themselves.

Firstly we were called 'savages'. After that, 'natives'. Then an undignified aboriginal with a small 'a'. Capital 'A' for Aboriginal was next, then Koori, which was supposed to mean all Aboriginal people in Australia, but which is a name specific to Aboriginal groups in New South Wales and some Aboriginal groups in Victoria. Then last but not least 'indigenous'.

Through all these name changes, two hundred odd years have elapsed. During that time we have been prodded, poked, poisoned, tested, examined, written about, Aboriginal skulls taken across to the other side of the world for observation . . . Could we possibly be the missing link scientists since Darwin have been searching for, to connect humans to the apes?

We are the most studied group of people in the world. We were, and still are, just numbers and statistics, because of this scientific research – yet another white industry living off the black community. There are statistics and probability studies that monitor every aspect of an Aboriginal person's life – our life expectancy, our infant mortality, our probability of dying once in custody. The list is endless. Technology is making the brain bigger than the heart. All these facts and figures allow white people to avoid facing the reality that we are human beings, we are families, we are people who grieve for the loss of our loved ones.

To break this cycle, attitudes have to change at every level. What is true for the young children – they have to learn how to ask questions and listen if they are going to understand about Aboriginal culture – is true for the adults running this country. The difference is, the adults never learnt this when they were at school. The government bureaucrats and politicians have visions of what is right for us. Our vision of what is right for us is not listened to. We are always told what is good for us but never asked.

I remember when my brother Paul's case was being considered for inclusion in the Royal Commission into Aboriginal Deaths in Custody. There were six cases that were being considered in Victoria. The families of the boys who died gathered together for a meeting and were asked to propose a plan that would help avoid any more people dying in custody. The families all got together and worked out recommendations of how to stop the deaths.

When these recommendations were given to the Commission, they turned around and said it would cost too much money to implement them. In comparison to the money spent in lawyers' fees to run the Commission, which ran into millions of dollars and resulted in virtually none of the Commission's recommendations being acted upon, what we were proposing was chicken feed. They then proceeded to tell us what would be better for us and less costly. But we knew what it was going to cost. More lives.

Larry Walsh took part in those meetings. His brother had died in custody in Bendigo. Since I first met Larry I connected with him. I met him through Paul. He's got a very powerful spirit and plays an important role in many communities around Victoria. His knowledge of the Aboriginal cultures of Victoria is really thorough. He's like an institution all in himself.

Larry describes better than I can some of the factors that contribute to the decision to take your own life. These are the things that were never really understood by the Royal Commission or by most of the 'experts'. He says:

They keep trying to bandaid the problem and people keep on dying. The real problem is to do with making you feel you don't belong in your own place. Forty-three of the initial ninety-nine deaths investigated by the Royal Commission were stolen-generation people – people taken away from their families when they were young kids. When this has happened to you, for the rest of your life you feel out of place.

Then there is how people were treated by the police, not just in the jail. You see, there are some fears that you can face and they go away. The fear of the cops is different. You can try and face that fear but you know there is nothing you can do about it because they've had control over you all your life. That kind of fear gets you. That got to Paul and to many others. That feeling that you can't win. That fear stays in you until it is too much.

What the families suggested to the Royal Commission was to have an Aboriginal person available to go into the jails as soon as someone is picked up. This was one recommendation to try and deal with this fear. We wanted that to become policy. Instead it was made a standing order, which means it is at the discretion of the police to implement. And, of course, they don't have to let anyone know. Many's the time they say, 'Oh, we didn't know he was Aboriginal', and so it goes on.

Many of the recommendations were not even tried. Then in the years following the Royal Commission the number of deaths in custody was increasing at such a rate that the government had to re-evaluate and, through the state governments, reconsider what the Aboriginal communities had suggested.

One thing that has been tried with a lot of success is for the Aboriginal communities to set up 'dry-out' centres. Instead of people being put straight into jail for minor offences like drinking, they could go to these centres. Two years after setting up some of these programs with the communities, the government changes and the funds are cut again. We're back to square one.

Even when the white bureaucracy does take up an idea from the community, they might like the idea, but then they have to make it fit with guidelines and conditions and 'performance indicators', so that eventually what comes out is no longer what the community is suggesting. For example, they might say 'yes' to a suggestion 'provided there is a qualified counsellor'. The best qualified person to do the job in the Aboriginal community probably hasn't got the qualifications from the white society and vice versa. The way a community measures success and the way white bureaucracy measures success can be completely different.

A hundred years ago in my culture, the worst thing you could do to me would be to isolate me from my own community. Separation is still one of the worst punishments in many communities. People think we're talking about laws that were operating two hundred years ago. For many, many Aboriginal people this is still the way of living today.

Often it is the white people's belief that we are the same as them culturally that stands in the way of them understanding the differences. They think they've made us live the same as them for two hundred years so we must be the same by now. This is not so. We don't like to be separated or isolated. We don't like to be forcibly enclosed. The European is scared of wide open places. These wide open places are where we are at home. We still have these differences in spite of the last two hundred years.

Even our own people, sometimes, when they join the bureaucracy, even when they know who they are and where they come from, they start operating like the whiteman wants them to.

Another recommendation was that money be put aside for counselling of the families and the communities of those who died in custody. I don't know of any family that got money for counselling. Many families are still destroyed because of these deaths. Members of those families keep suffering and keep dying before their time. A family and community who loses someone in this way feels that pain deeply. No one is getting any help to deal with that pain.

Sometimes I wonder if any Europeans understand those close links Aboriginal families have with each other. I have a suspicion that a lot of the follow-on deaths would not be happening if people understood these close family links and there was counselling to help families heal.

To be fair, Aboriginal families find it difficult to speak about these deaths amongst themselves. You don't like to speak about the dead – 'let their spirit rest'. I say, 'How can a spirit rest that died in such a horrific way, so violently?' But that's me you see. I question these things. The fact that culturally we can't discuss the dead easily, makes it hard to deal with. We have to face up to the fact that we have to break a tradition or a taboo to deal with what is happening to us now. These traditions were around when we were never faced with the horror of the way our people have died since the Invasion. This is why someone from outside the family who is not bound by the same taboo is needed to help families through this trauma. This is what was recommended to the Royal Commission ten years ago. I don't know of any family that has been given this help.

It's true, isn't it, that in any catastrophe that involves the death of people on such a scale as our people have suffered, the need for counselling is a matter of course. For Aboriginal families this has never been recognised.

One of the recommendations Larry talks about was tried in Kuranda, inland from Cairns, where a lot of my relations live. The Aboriginal community got together to form a night patrol. People on a volunteer basis take out a bus at closing time for the pubs and make sure their people get home off the streets. The rate of Aboriginal people in custody dropped dramatically as soon as this program began. In the words of one of the young men involved in the volunteer patrol, 'The town calmed down. Things were good. But the resources needed to support the program, for petrol, to keep the bus serviced and going, aren't there. The police make it difficult rather than working in with us for the good of us all.'

My mum and dad are members of a newly formed social justice group called Yubana Ooloma Council of Elders – that means old man-old woman council. The Department of Aboriginal Affairs Family Services approached a group of elders to volunteer to work with young Aboriginal kids to reduce the juvenile crime rate.

The elders take groups of young offenders and kids on the street out on camps and teach them how to make spears and go hunting. The kids have to hunt for their tucker and cook it. My mum says:

> We're hoping that this will help give them back pride in their culture and realise what there is out there to learn. Instead of that attitude that has been drummed into them, 'You're black, stand back.' It's going to be a hard job, but we're hoping it will have an effect on a lot of things like the numbers of deaths in custody and all these problems.

Often community programs are started and then given so few resources that they fail. If they succeeded, then the problems would begin to be solved and that would mean a lot of white people would be out of work. The Minister for Aboriginal Affairs has always been a whiteman. So are the majority of other people paid to be in charge of the affairs of Aboriginal people. Our own people should be in these positions of power, taking care of ourselves. We have the education and the knowledge of our people to do this. The white system of government is keeping our young people out on the streets and giving them no hope of any jobs or any future because they see their aunties and uncles and cousins with no jobs and no hope.

I'm spending more time at home now. The loss of my brother Paul left a big hole. He used to come back home all the time with great ideas of things to do to motivate the kids on Yarrabah, and get people excited about learning the dances and being proud to remember the culture.

'Have faith in yourself,' he would say. 'Don't let these whitefullas take anything else from you. Keep your head up and don't walk three steps behind. Stand up straight and walk three steps in front.' I've deleted a few expletives! He was passionate about keeping what we have left and when it came time to stand up and be counted, he was the first in line. That's the reason he was always singled out by the police on Yarrabah. He would never back down.

Because of Paul's training in theatre – he trained for three years in professional theatre at the Victorian College of the Arts Drama School – he had a positive way of bringing people together. He used to say that theatre was such a good way to get our message across because it made people laugh and have a good time, as well as think of the issues that need looking at. He was the one in the family that was learning to be the keeper of our culture and who would then teach everybody else. Losing him meant that I had to step into this position, but I wasn't quite ready because I was still bound up in learning the other side. That was what I was teaching him. How to handle the migaloo ways in the city.

There are many dancers and didjeridoo players that are better than me but who are stuck in the position of still being overseen by a white system that keeps them in their place. I see this all the time when I go up home. Especially in one major company, where these really talented dancers are being used to entertain the endless stream of tourists that flock to North Queensland. As well as working long hours, they are struggling to get paid a basic wage.

Companies like this one are making millions of dollars each year from the sale of our culture. The people who are making it are the white people. The dancers and their elders are kept poor, under control, and fearful of losing the little they have if they go against the white management. When they speak up and question how much they are paid, or the conditions they are working under, then, just like their ancestors, they are labelled as troublemakers. In the old days they would be chained and shipped off to another reserve. Now they are sacked and eventually have to find work, if they can, away from their culture, working at jobs they don't want to do. They usually end up on the grog to try and forget the insanity of this situation – losing the job of presenting their own culture.

Most of the dancers and performers I am talking about are more talented than me, but because of what I have learnt from going away from home, I am in a position where I can speak my mind and be in control of my own work. It depresses me when I go home and see the frustration and hopelessness in the eyes of my people, who have all this beautiful culture to give and yet are being ripped off every way they turn. It is still too hard for me to come back home to live because I would be back in this system, too. It's not that I'm smarter, it's just that I went away and learnt how to play their game. I'm still learning.

Like Budda Paul before me, now I try and bring home messages of hope. One trip home, I took this group of trainee teachers up to the Laura Aboriginal Dance and Cultural Festival, run by the Ang-Gnarra Aboriginal Corporation. About thirty different Aboriginal groups from all across the top of Australia come and dance for two days. On the way up this time, we stopped at my Uncle Peter and Aunty Milda's place in Ingham. My aunty always likes us to ring up before arriving so she can have damper and a cup of tea ready.

While we were having a cuppa, Aunty Milda pulled me over to the corner. The old people've got a way to talk to you. When they want you for anything they have gestures and sounds to get your attention. You know when them fullas want you to talk or be quiet. So I went over to my aunty and said, 'Yeah, Aunty?' She goes, 'Who them fullas there?' I said, 'Aah, these fullas are teachers.' And she said, 'You gonna take them up?' And I said, 'Yeah.' She said, 'Why do them fullas come up here for?' I said, 'Well, Aunty, they want to come up to see black-fullas dancing and they want to hear about our spiritual land and ah . . .' She said, 'What, there no blackfullas down there?' 'Yeah, they got a lot of blackfullas down there but it's a little bit different, you know.' She said, 'What they been come all the way up here to see us blackfullas for?' And I said, 'Yeeah, well . . . not just to see us, as in blackfullas, well, I suppose that too, but to sort of see what we do, as in dancing and singing and painting. And it just happens that we've got two days of this festival.' She said, 'Gee, hey, that's a long way to come, eh? They come a long way just to see us, don't they?'

That brought tears to my eyes because she couldn't believe that white people, even from overseas, would come all this way just to see black people. In her day, white people came up here to round us up and put us on reserves and even kill us. Now, she's got these young fullas having a cup of tea and damper with her, asking all these questions and wanting to know more about her people. Uncle Peter said as we left, 'You people you goin' to have a good time up there, you know.'

This friend of mine, Ron, who is a church man and someone who really searches deeply to understand his relationship with Aboriginal culture, came up home for the Laura Festival with his whole family. All of them wanted to experience what it was like to be at this Aboriginal dance festival. On the way up to Laura, we stopped at my relations as usual and they got to meet lots of my family. The other day, back in Melbourne, Ron told me:

It surprises me. When I read stories of what has happened to Aboriginal people in this country I'm very moved. And you know what? I find that I can't remember the stories. Often it's the story that has moved me the most that I just can't remember. It is like something is blocking my memory. Maybe

157

it is something in my own upbringing that wants to forget these things.

That really took me by surprise. But it made a lot of sense of how white people react to us. It made me think too of what this wonderful man, Michael Timpano from Canada, said to me. He also came up to the Laura Festival to find out about Aboriginal people. He said:

I thought I'd be the only white man there. I thought I'd feel out of place, uncomfortable. I can honestly say, when we passed that gate, that entrance to the sacred grounds, not once did I feel out of place. Never. And I was introduced to tons of people.

I thought to myself, 'Hey, I'm a white man here. I'm the one who should be feeling uncomfortable.' These people are not uncomfortable around white people. I think it's that us white people are uncomfortable around them. Like I said, I thought I would be out of place but they never let me feel uncomfortable.

Meme's son, Joe, was thirteen when he came up to the Laura Festival. He was really wary about coming up. He's got really blond hair and blue eyes, and he kept saying to his mum, 'Look at me. They'll never accept me up there.' I knew I'd only have to introduce him to my nephews and he'd be right.

That first morning, I was looking for him. I saw this whole mob of kids chasing the footy around, dust flying, legs and arms going everywhere. There in the middle of them was this streak of white hair. I could hear the other fullas yelling out, 'Go, Joe, go, Joey, go!' He and Ron's boys, Nick and David, were out there running up and down that patch of dirt from dawn till dusk. All ages, all colours, chasing the one ball.

Other times when I go home I like to show all my family, including my aunties, uncles and cousins, all the letters and drawings that the school kids, both primary and secondary, send me. We sit down and read them all. They are really amazed and say, 'Aaah, well, wow.' My cousin Trevor Pryor, or Boxhead – that's his nickname – said one day after he'd read a great pile of letters, 'What, is this white kids writing this?' And I said, 'Well, all sorts of kids, from all different backgrounds.' And he said, 'That's deadly, eh?'

Some of these letters would blow you out of the water. The beauty in the hearts of some of these students sucks the breath out of me. To have my family see what these students are thinking, and that's often just after one contact with one Aboriginal person, that gives us all hope. As I've said before, we need white people to heal, for us to heal, see? These young people are the light.

Children always seem to bridge the gap. Like music, if you listen to them and follow their lead, your spirit will dance.

'Hey, I've been to Yarrabah,' this little one yelled out

at the top of her voice. I was right in the middle of explaining where I come from to a class. I said, 'Oh! Hello! Well, that's my mob there.' And she said, 'Gee, it's beautiful there.' And I said, 'Who did you know out there?' And she said, 'Oh, we met a lot of people there.'

I was interested how she got to Yarrabah. She said she was down on the Esplanade in Cairns and she met this old lady. She went up and sat down and started talking to her. There are always articles in the local paper about all the drunk Aboriginals down on the Esplanade. How they are putting off the tourists and shouldn't be allowed to be there. This little one was only seven or so. She told me she went up to the old lady and started talking to her and the old woman said, 'Aah, my girl, sit down and have a chat.' And her mum and dad, they were fine, they ended up sitting down and joining this little mob. The old lady asked, 'You fullas want to come over to Yarrabah?'

They ended up spending the whole day over there. They had cups of tea and saw all around Yarrie and the young girl played with all the kids.

That's all it takes. That's all it takes, just to sit down and talk and listen to each other.

NO MATTER WHERE YOU ARE

*It overawes me that these birds will come out and dance
with you even over the other side of the world.*

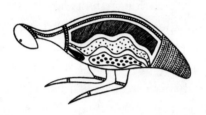

A long time ago, Aboriginal people had the closest
thing to a sixth sense. But it wasn't perceived of in
numbers, with a box around each sense and labelled
one to six. There were none of the influences of modern life, like television and video games, to take the
edge off your senses. Your senses were totally tuned to
the world around you. They had to be if you were
going to survive.

Like where I come from, the rainforest people used to
whistle like the birds and they could communicate with
them. They would listen to each other because there was
nothing in the way to stop that listening. Now it's a lot
harder.

The drugs and the alcohol introduced to my
people have blurred this line of communication.

My Aunty Val says:

Our nonverbal communication is very strong. Deep down things are passed on. In the old days you had to know these things to be safe. Something would happen in the atmosphere around you and I remember all us kids would go quiet. You would watch your parents for signs. Kids were very alert in those days. You didn't have to yell at kids much then. There weren't many words said. With my first couple of kids, I could direct them by looking at them or with a gesture of my hand. With my younger ones I lost this nonverbal communication because we were living more and more in the migaloo way.

This nonverbal communication between us is not something out of a weird dream. It just goes back to the wisdom and the strength that is given from the earth itself. The earth that you walk on, that flies around in the air, that is rained on, that gives strength to things that grow, that other things eat, that are then eaten by us so we can live. The earth cradles the rain when it falls from the sky for us to drink and bathe in, and it's the same earth that you become part of when you die.

The strength and the power of the earth is important for all people. Through a connection with the earth, you feel a part of the cycle of life and death and you know your place within that cycle at any point in time.

It doesn't matter how much technology and science we develop, we will never break nature's cycle. We are born and live, then eventually die along with all other living things. We all end up back in the earth.

However blurred this sense of communication has become, most Aboriginal people have a strong belief in animals as messengers, especially birds.

I'd just been dancing the Kite-Hawk Dance at this school. I always ask the students, especially if it's a bush school, if any of them have seen the kite hawk. It amazes me how many of them just look blank. There'll only be two or three that put their hand up. I joke with them, 'Then all you fullas here must walk round with your heads down looking for money on the ground.' They all crack up, too.

Driving home this day, I saw a kite hawk out of the corner of my eye. We were travelling along a two-lane freeway. Right opposite this stretch of road was where I'd done a corroboree with the Mona Mona boys from Kuranda up north, three years before. These boys can really shake-a-leg, especially Bertie Riley. His father, Lance, is a very respected elder of the Tjapukai people. When I saw the kite hawk and looked across, I said to my friend Meme, 'This is right where the corroboree took place in Turong Park. Isn't that amazing.' We pulled over and jumped out and I said, 'We'll have a look, eh?'

This kite hawk that was flying along stopped a couple of times, hovered, then came straight over right next to the car. Just hovered there. It didn't go away. And then its partner – brother, sister, partner, whatever – came across and hovered right above it. It was double-decker kite hawks right there, just six metres above us to the right. They stayed there for maybe five or ten minutes.

It humbles you seeing the kite hawks. They seem to be saying, 'Don't forget. Don't forget. Don't forget us.' And I think, when I see that, I don't forget. You know why you're here. You know why you're not dead. It's probably a message from them telling you. A lot of people look at it and say it's weird. But I look at it and say it's a message from the old people saying 'Keep going'. For me that's what it means.

These birds, these kite hawks, talk to me even when I travel right over the other side of the world. You wouldn't believe that, would you? Only about seven years ago, when I was forty, I went overseas for the first time. I went to Bristol, in England, to visit my godson Ciaran's uncle and aunty. I mentioned before about making friends during my DJing days at the Albion Charles. One very beautiful person that I have stayed friends with ever since is Ciaran's mother, Mari. Her sister, Margaret Ward, is an Irish historian and has written two biographies on Irish women. Her partner, Paddy Hillyard, is an academic interested in civil liberties and human rights and he also writes books on these subjects.

While I was there, I ended up performing at their children, Medbh and Fintan's, school. By the time we got back to their house after the performance, there were phone calls from three more schools interested in me visiting them. At one school they had just completed a small course on Aboriginal culture, which included videos and books on Dreamtime stories. So, for them, it was as though I had stepped out of the books and off the screen and into their classroom. By the time I had finished my shows at these schools, parents from two of the schools wanted a performance. Their idea was, why should the kids have all the fun? And it might be a long time between drinks before they see another Aboriginal person.

After painting up at Paddy and Margaret's house, we all jumped in this little car and headed off to the park. My presence is still felt in the car because I left paint all over the upholstery. Paddy knew of one gum tree that was just around the corner so we pulled up and I jumped out, climbed up and along this wall which was about two and a half metres high to get these gum leaves. There I am, standing up on this wall, my judda jah on, paint all over me, like a beacon in the night, but this was in the daytime, and still nobody noticed.

The parents and children were waiting when we arrived. There was lots of bushland, walking tracks, and not too far away, behind safety fences, there was a big drop down to the River Avon. This parkland is called Clifton Downs. It was Paddy's idea to perform here overlooking the gorge. It was really beautiful. The biggest plus was that it was summer. I wouldn't be game enough to run around over there in my judda jah in winter. I'd freeze my big black dot off!

I've got the leaves and I'm doing some dances, all the

time explaining about their meanings. Then it came to the Kite-Hawk Dance, which I explained first, then danced, shook my legs and hovered like a kite hawk. After that it was their turn. While I was singing and doing the dance with them they all stopped, pointed to the air above me and yelled, 'Look!' As I looked around, there were two kite hawks that sat only about three, four metres above me, over my shoulder. I was still clapping the sticks, and the birds' heads slowly turned as they watched us dance. While they hovered above, it seemed like they couldn't believe their eyes. The feeling was mutual. They stayed there for twenty or thirty seconds. You could hear the whoosh of their wings as they both flew off.

We finished the dance and as the parents and children were sitting down, Paddy said, 'You can tell 'em anything you want now and they would believe it!' I said, 'Gee, I'm really glad I didn't do the snake dance.'

It overawes me that these birds will come out – some people may think it's twilight zone material, call it what you want – but these birds came out and danced with us. And this was over the other side of the world from where this dance belongs.

As I watched the birds, I thought of my brother Paul. He could really dance. He often busked in the centre of the city back in Melbourne, usually in the Bourke Street Mall. One day he asked me to meet him for lunch. He gave me a time, one o'clock, but knowing my brother is like knowing myself and I knew he meant blackfulla time: anytime from one o'clock till four o'clock in the afternoon would be on time. You see, for us fullas there is a right time to do everything but it is not necessarily according to the clock. Time itself tells us when to do what we have to do.

I made my way into the city and got to the mall about one-thirty. No sign of Paul anywhere. All I could see was a big mob of people. There must have been about five or six hundred people gathered around something happening. I decided to see what was going on that would make so many people make so much noise and keep them interested on their lunchbreak. I pushed my way through the crowd and right in the middle, all by himself, was this skinny little blackfulla dancing.

I got myself into a good position and watched his show. He had everybody mesmerised. He was being the kangaroo, hopping around the edge of the circle of people. He came to a stop and pretended to feed in front of this little boy who was sitting on his mother's lap. The little boy said, 'Mummy, Mummy, can I feed the kangaroo?' His mother looked at him and said, 'No, darling, he's not a kangaroo, he's a man pretending to be a kangaroo.' The boy looked back up with his big, wide eyes and said, 'Can I feed him anyway?'

I never think of myself as a great dancer like Paul. So, when these kite hawks keep coming out when I dance it really surprises me. If I was a good dancer I wouldn't be so surprised. But, you see, it is these dances and songs that I am learning now that are bringing this communication with the other living things back to me.

Because I'm not a traditional person in the sense that most of my living is in the city, I used to wonder if I'd lost this special connection. There is a lot of our culture that has been taken away. It's not so much that we've lost it. We haven't lost it. Lost is like saying we misplaced it. We never misplaced it. It was taken away and destroyed. It's always been there. And we've always fought to keep it. But when I see the kite hawks, it makes me realise that I, too, have this something special now.

Being a blackfulla, you don't really question what this power is. You say, 'It's there. It happened. I have it.' Spiritual events like these are the things that keep us connected. They can happen anywhere and anytime.

Jaii, Paul's son, moved to Sydney from the country not long ago. He moved there by himself and was staying in a hostel. He's only fifteen. He was feeling pretty lonely one time and was trying to make contact with a relation that lived on the other side of Sydney. He couldn't make contact so, anyway, this day he just decided to get on the train and head in that direction. He had no money, nothing, and didn't know where he was going.

When the train he was on passed through Redfern – an inner-city suburb where a lot of Aboriginal people live – this blackfulla got on and sat down next to him. They got talking. Straightaway the fulla asked him his name. As soon as he said Pryor, this bloke jumped up and said, 'You not from the Pryor mob from Townsville?' Jaii said, 'Yeah.' And this bloke said, 'You must know Paul Pryor from up there?' 'Yeah, he's my dad.' The fulla jumped up and grabbed him and hugged him and told him he knew his father well. Ended up, this fulla looked after him, made sure he had somewhere to stay and gave him some money. His mother Maggie says, 'I knew I didn't have to worry about him any more. His father's spirit is looking after him.'

These special moments, like with Jaii on the train and with the kite hawks flying over you, that's when you know you are not alone and you have a purpose.

Paul used to always say about the didjeridoo:

> This stick, it got a spirit of its own. You don't even have to play it and people listen. They see you with it, they come straight up to you and ask you all about it. This stick here can get your foot in the door of a lot of people's hearts and minds. It's got the power to do that.

People would ask him to play and he would say, 'Sure. But first of all I'll tell you this.' And then he would tell them all about us blackfullas. He was clever like that.

The magic of the didjeridoo goes beyond people. I was up in the Blue Mountains doing this show. It was a very small primary school. I'm doing the performance and talking and joking and having a really good time.

Then it came to the didjeridoo. I have a special space within the performance to teach them about sniffing and squirting at the same time, which is my way of teaching circular breathing.

I start playing. Everyone likes the kookaburra, so the first one I do is the kookaburra. While I was doing this, out through the windows – they were like louvres – high up on the right-hand side of the classroom, all of a sudden, maybe about four to six kookaburras flew down and landed on the tree. They started 'hoohooohaahaaa-haahaa'. I kept going on the didj. The kids, they looked at me and then they looked at the end of the didjeridoo. They were mesmerised. Then their eyes drifted up to where the kookaburras were, then drifted back down again to the end of the stick. They went, 'Wow! How did he do that?!'

I stopped doing the kookaburra and when I looked up at these ones sitting up in the tree they had their heads tilted on the side as if to say, 'Who's that fake down there?' When I blew on the didj again, they started 'hoohoohaahaahaahaa', making cackling sounds. And the kids went, 'Wow!' At any rate, finally, the kookaburras flew off. It was good fun. I was a bit amazed but I just continued on with the show. The kids were all sitting up straight and the teacher said, 'That was an interesting little trick.'

After I finished the show, I walked out to have a chat with the teachers. They asked me, 'Come on, really and truly, you had a bunch of kookaburras stuck in your boot and you let 'em out on cue, didn't you?' I said, 'No. They belong to you mob. They're from up here.' 'Yeah, right mate!' they said. They wouldn't believe me. They thought I had kookaburras in the boot of my car, Rusty!

You can't explain the feeling that comes over you when this happens. Sometimes, I shrug it off, not wanting to examine it. But to tell you the truth, I was aware of their sound following me all the way up to the school that day. During the first half of the show they were sounding off in the distance. Then as I came up to presenting the didjeridoo, they went quiet. When I began, they joined in. The kookaburras sitting outside the windows laughing was magic.

Special moments like this soften the hard times – when you need to feel something good, to make the bad feelings go away.

Around the time that my nephew Liam died, I went back to visit a school that I had done a week at the year before, St Dominics Priory in Adelaide. I dropped in on the kinders. Nobody knew I was coming. I had a day free and felt like dropping in for a cup of tea. I snuck up to where the kinders were and just walked straight in through the door. They were busily doing something to a little tree in the middle of the classroom.

This little one just raced up and had this look on her face that will stay with me forever. She screamed excitedly, 'Look, look, you're here, you're here! I just made a wish and stuck it on the tree and you're here!' She wrapped herself around me and hugged me. Then all of a sudden, the whole class full of kids wrapped them-selves around me.

When I looked at the teacher she was standing there in disbelief. She'd been working with them on a wishing tree and the children had to write down their wish and stick it on the tree. This little one had just stuck hers on the tree. 'I wish Monty would come back and visit.' What do I do? Appear. I felt like a black Santa.

As an Aboriginal person, you know when you are around people who don't like you because you are black. You've got to understand that the reason for this is because of their lack of awareness through a lack of learning. What-ever knowledge they have had, it's been wrong.

What you have to do as a black person, so you don't get hurt physically or mentally, is to work hard at achiev-ing stability within yourself. Then you have to work hard at achieving stability within the minds of these people who have this lack of knowledge. To achieve this stabil-ity you have to start somewhere. That starting point is within yourself.

The same has to happen on a national level. Recon-ciliation has to start from within yourself.

For me, reconciliation means you start at day one, Invasion Day. All of us have to start at this point and take the journey hand in hand through our history, looking at what has happened along the way, savouring the good times and learning from the bad times. We have to admit to ourselves and each other that certain events did happen in our history together. The past is still here with us. We have to acknowledge the past so we can understand and accept it and then go on, move on from there into a better future.

How can you reconcile something that has never been fully acknowledged or understood? There has been enough avoidance: 'It happened two hundred years ago', 'we didn't do it', 'it's not my fault', 'you should have got over it by now'. Sticking your head in the sand won't solve the problem. It only holds us back. Admitting we have a black and white history will be the first step towards healing this nation.

A cousin of mine went to a public meeting in Mareeba on the Atherton Tableland in far north Queensland. There were a couple of families of black people there and a lot of whitefullas. The talk swung around to saying that everyone should forget about what happened in the past and we have to just look to the future.

My cousin got up and spoke. He has a very good way with words. He talked about Anzac Day and how it is commemorated every year. 'Lest We Forget.' He asked the white people there how they would feel if it was suggested to forget Anzac Day. There was silence. Then he pointed out that it is the same for black people remembering the massacres and atrocities of the past. When he sat down the whole audience applauded him.

We Aboriginal people have got to make sure that we

173

give non-Aboriginal people the information in a way that will make them discover for themselves what has gone on. I don't know if it was at that same meeting, but one old fulla got up and said, 'You migaloos change your laws like you change your undies!'

Aboriginal people don't understand the instability of laws. It is very unsettling, this instability. One moment the whitefulla government talks about Mabo and Wik, and the need to acknowledge the traditional owners' entitlement of access to their land, what they call Native Title. Next, they want it all changed again and there's another plan. When the final decision was being made on Mabo, it was noted in the summary papers that seven hundred and forty-eight different pieces of legislation governing Aboriginal people's lives had been made in the two hundred and eight years of whitefulla rule. Seven hundred and forty-eight! There has got to be a knowledge of stability if people are to feel secure in themselves.

For us, law was passed on over thousands of years. No culture is static, but for Aboriginal people there was a stability of knowing your land and your people and where you belonged. Although there were wars between tribes, we were not a colonising people. Why would you go and conquer someone else's land when that is not your spirit? You would feel bad about taking someone's place when it doesn't belong to you. It would be bad for your spirit.

174

When Cathy Freeman took the Aboriginal and Australian flags out at the 1995 Commonwealth Games and joined them as one, she made the whole of Australia stand up and look at ourselves. A lot of people don't realise what she had to fight against in order to achieve winning a gold medal in the 400 metres. What she was doing with the two flags was saying, 'I'm proud to be an Aboriginal Australian.' There was some negative feedback but a lot of positive response to her symbolic act of uniting our country on such an international stage. I don't think Cathy realised the impact she would have. Maybe in the next thirty to forty or fifty years we, as a nation, might realise the great contribution she made in terms of provoking an understanding of ourselves by bringing our two flags together.

What reconciliation has to achieve is a state of mutual respect. There are examples of this happening between individuals and small groups right across the country and this gives us all great hope.

I really like this story the secretary at a Sydney school told me. The story happened in a small town in Western Australia. This whitefulla was like Tim the Toolman. All his tools had designated places in his toolshed where they had to be put. He had outlines of each tool so there could be no mistake where each tool had its resting place. No one could lay a hand on anything within the boundary of his toolshed, not even his wife. One morning he went out the back and discovered that all the resting places were empty, leaving only the marked spaces where once his tools had been.

He was a respected man within the community and he let it be known to everyone in the neighbourhood how upset he was. It was common knowledge locally that there was a bunch of little blackfullas nicking stuff over back fences. Instead of going to the police, the Toolman went to the local elders and made this statement: 'You have your sacred sites, I have my toolshed. I want my tools back.' The next day all the tools were back in his shed.

You get a clear perspective on these things from a distance sometimes. In 1995, I found myself in Crossmaglen, Northern Ireland. I was asked to give a paper on deaths in custody at the 23rd Annual Conference held by the European Group for the Study of Deviance and Social Control.

I first flew to Dublin, then got on a train to Dundalk, where I was picked up by car and driven to Crossmaglen on the border. They call it 'sniper country', which did away with any thoughts I had in my mind of going for early morning runs. I had an excuse to sleep in.

The conference was held in a hall only ninety metres from the huge Glassdrummond base. The first things I noticed were the gun towers, the forts, and the helicopter gunships flying over all the time. The whole countryside is criss-crossed with laser beams that are emitted from the gun towers. Cameras follow your every move. In a playing field, right beside the gun towers of the most militarised frontier in Europe, young children were playing their Gaelic football and the Irish game of hurling as if there was not a worry in the world.

As a visitor, I knew I had things to worry about. The first thing I had to worry about was carrying my didjeridoos around. I wondered why this fulla carrying my didjeridoo took off real fast and got inside the hall. The hall was about thirty metres from the gun tower. Here's this two-metre-long parcel, bundled up with tape all over it. I knew what it was – just a couple of hollow sticks – but them fullas in the gun tower didn't know. Even though it was a cease-fire at that time, there is always room for a misunderstanding.

People had come from all over Europe to give papers at the conference. Everyone was an academic except one little blackfulla from Australia. Academic fullas speak a whole different language, but after a couple of pints of stout, their speech patterns become a little clearer.

When I was asked to give the paper, I was a bit confused on how to present it. My cousin Henrietta Fourmile is experienced in doing this, so I contacted her. She has always been a great inspiration to me with all the work she has done in the academic field for our people. At the moment she is in Canada working with the Indigenous Committee of the United Nations looking into cultural biodiversity and intellectual property rights for indigenous people throughout the world. This is the area of study she is concentrating on for her Masters as well. She advised me to write down notes for my speech. When the time came to give my paper, I never looked at it once, because there were only a few solitary words on an almost blank sheet of paper.

I came to the end of my talk, which included a video about my brother Paul that a current affairs TV program had prepared after his death. There was a big round of applause and people came up and hugged me and shook my hand. They kept asking me for a copy of my paper. I told them I could go over all the things I had spoken about again but the only paper I had was the one in my head. They all understood that I spoke from my heart, they could see things in my eyes and they listened to my words but, being academics, they had to have a paper in their hand to make them feel they'd understood. My friend said, 'This time their head was the fax machine and the paper was sent orally.'

I had tasted Guinness back in Australia but it tasted nothing like it did here. The locals kept telling me it doesn't travel well. At the end of the conference there was a dance. I found I was pretty good at doing Irish dancing, at least I thought I was, but it could have been the three or four pints of Guinness I'd had, and that was the most I'd ever drunk, but these fullas kept sticking it under your nose all the time.

I played didjeridoo, then sat down and listened to this wonderful man thanking everybody for coming to Crossmaglen and talking about the importance of his people keeping the culture that is theirs. He finished by saying, 'They'll not take away our language. They'll not take away our songs. They'll not take away our sport.'

While he was saying these words, the gunships were flying overhead. I was thinking, well, we've got to worry about the bullymen, the police, but at least they don't fly overhead with machine guns all the time. My heart was happy but also sad after seeing these children and their elders in such adversity being able to stand up and be so strong.

It was arranged that I visit Belfast. Paula MacManus, a woman at the conference, invited me to stay at her place in anticipation of me performing in schools. Her father was a school principal and through his contacts it wasn't long before I had several shows booked. The emotions I had about going to Belfast were confusing. On one hand you have the stories of leprechauns, potatoes, Van Morrison, the beautiful green country-side, burning peat moss, and the Harland and Wolff Dockyard where the Titanic was built. Then, suddenly, here you are driving through this city barricaded up, hardly a glass window to be seen through, being told stories of where bombs were let off and people were shot, military outposts, and the whole place divided down religious lines.

Going to Ireland was an eye-opener. Because of the complexities that are woven into the structure of the society as it is now, it is very hard for outsiders to under-stand. The oppression that has been happening there has been happening for over eight hundred years and because of this, it's going to take a very long time to heal. I think I could see the similarities with what happened in my country but the good thing is that our situation has only happened in the last two hundred or so years.

What I learnt and what I felt in Ireland was the magnificent strength and resilience of these people. I saw so much pain and so much happiness, so much strength and so much love and so much laughter living amongst all this destruction and sorrow.

It reminded me a lot of us.

The Irish people I met there fight hard to keep strong through their language, song and dance. I was invited to speak at the Language Centre in Belfast. There, the students speak their native tongue of Gaelic all the time. So, I said, 'Okay, that's great but I only know a little bit of my own language, no Gaelic, only English. What do I do?' They said that as a guest it was all right for me to speak in English. So, I sang and danced, told stories in blackfulla talk. They understood every word. I got them to chant, they sang and clapped and wouldn't let me leave the stage. They wanted to hear stories about Aboriginal people, good things, bad things, where we are in our struggle. After the performance, they talked about getting an Aboriginal dance group to visit Ireland.

From what I saw and felt, our histories were similar in that we were both storytellers and passed on oral history. Our songs and dances kept us strong as did theirs. The British Empire sought to conquer without any understanding of this.

Visiting the offices of Sinn Fein, I've got to say, was an

awesome experience in itself. I felt so humbled to be right in the engine room of these people's struggle for survival. This one man I met in the office had one arm, the other was just a stump. One eye was missing and he had this terrible limp. He had this beautiful smile across his face as I was telling him about Aboriginal people. Very diplomatically, I was trying to find out a way to ask him how he ended up like he was. He said a bomb blew his arm off at the elbow, in prison someone poked his eye out with a screwdriver, and the police smashed his kneecaps. He finished off by saying, 'Aye, I guess I'm just lucky!'

I think seeing people in that situation is an inspiration. We've only had a short term of this kind of treatment in Australia. We have more of an opportunity to make this such a wonderful, absolutely brilliant, beautiful place. In Australia, we have the advantage of many more ethnic groups coming to our country from parts of Europe, the Middle East and Asia. They're the people that provided the labour to build just about every structure here. That started during the 1920s and 1930s.

We fought when the Invaders first stepped on our land. There were lots of wars that were not documented in white history. There were lots of lives lost that were never recorded. The fight for freedom and equality for Aboriginal people started to bring about some changes in the 1960s. There're still changes that have got to happen now. We have to look at what is missing, what is deficient within our society.

To be stronger together we have to look at our

181

strengths and weaknesses. The biggest weakness is the lack of recognition of Aboriginal people.

From Belfast to Balmain. I went back to visit a school that I had spent a week at, Nicholson Street Primary. I like to do that if I'm going past a school and I've got the time to drop in. As soon as I walked in, the little ones came racing over, grabbed my legs. There was lots of hugging and squeezing and everybody talking at once. After they settled down, we exchanged stories. Then I went into a class of older children and sat down. They were in the midst of singing 'The Purple People Eater'. Some played their recorders while others sang. When they had finished, I told them I used to sing that song when I was a little fulla, too. Not real little. Okay, then, I was a teenager. They laughed like anything.

The teacher asked me to sit down and said, 'And Monty has been somewhere really terrific. If you sit down and listen, Monty will tell you all about it.' 'Yes, thank you, teacher, for letting me come into your class. Well, kids, I've been to Ireland!' I said. They all went 'woooo'. So I said, 'Anyone know where Ireland is?' Some said yes. 'What about Dublin?' 'Yes, that's in Ireland.' 'England?' 'Yes, that's not too far away.'

Then I said, 'Do you know what happened when I went to Ireland? I went to Belfast. I was having a really good time working with some children there. Some of them were your age. I was interested in paintings they did on buildings. Some of them were really big, like murals. The Irish people were not unlike Aboriginal people. They used to tell stories through painting. They still do now and that was what these paintings were about.

'While I was taking photos of these murals, these children came up to me, probably about your age, maybe a little bit older. They started asking me questions in a Belfast accent. One of them asked, "And what country would you be from?" And I said, "Australia." And he looked at me and frowned and said, "But you're black!" And I said, "Well, yes, I know." And he said, "Do they have black people in Australia?" And I said, "Yes, of course. They've got all different sorts of people in Australia." And all those little Irish ones said, "oooh".

'Finally, I got back into the car and drove off. After a while, I realised why they thought like that. The two biggest TV shows from Australia that are shown in Ireland are "Neighbours" and "Home and Away". So, can anyone here tell me why those children over there would think that there weren't any black people living in Australia?'

One little boy, he was so intent on getting all the words out right, said, 'Well, um, on the . . . on the . . . on the shows . . . on "Neighbours" and "Home and Away", they only got one sorts of people there. They're . . . they're . . . they're all white people and all just one colour and nobody thinks that there is another colour, that there is other people here.' And I said, 'Yes, that's right, because there are Italians and Greeks and lots of different people here.' This other little bloke put his hand up, 'I'm Italian.' And then all the others started. 'And I'm Greek.' 'And I'm Irish.' I said, 'That's right, Australians are all sorts of people.'

I remember the day I finished the week in residence at this school. I was in this same class. This was the Friday and I said, 'Can any of you tell me what you've learnt from me being here?' One girl put her hand up and said, 'To respect the differences between people.'

It wasn't until I got the chance to go to Italy to perform at a festival near Friuli that I got to understand a lot about the difference between European culture and my culture.

I was in awe of the beauty of the buildings and their history. What most interested me in Italy was the difference between all the groups. If you were to say all Italians are the same, then you would insult a lot of people. It's true that they are all Italian, but the Romans are not the same as the Venetians, the Sicilians are not the same as the Calabrians, and so on. They all have their different dialects and customs. This made me think about ways of explaining the differences between Aboriginal groups to people of European heritage back here in Australia.

I played the didjeridoo and performed with my cousin Joe as part of the festival. We performed in this magnificent castle surrounded by a moat. After the performance, men and women came up and hugged and kissed me and pinched my cheeks, both sets.

While I was in Friuli, I met some people at the marketplace. We became friends. They showed me parts of their beautiful country. It felt good to be looked after by the locals. They were the people who took me to Venice, which is another place I had always dreamed of going to. Before I could drink in the rich beauty of this city, with its streets of water, I had to find out where Agent 007, James Bond, came up out of the water on his gondola-styled hovercraft and flew across the square. They laughed, 'Everybody wants to know that.'

I was amazed at the churches. Everything was steeped in rich cultural knowledge and it was on display everywhere, especially the religious side of things. By comparison, I imagined walking along the dry bed of the Finke River, the oldest river in the world, in the middle of Australia. In Italy, all the sacred sites are made by humans and are on show. You can feel things there, too.

In our culture back home, there is a feeling that you get from the spirit of a place. All you have to do is walk across the land and our history surrounds you. To a newcomer's eyes it might just look like bare land and rocks, but if someone who knows this place is to sit down with you and tell you its stories and secrets, that will open the eyes you need to see the land. Through these different eyes, you can see what the land has to give you.

You don't have to see physical structures to feel

awe-inspired. The stories that are told create images that surpass anything humans can make.

Sacred sites are scattered everywhere across Italy. They are known and well documented and are treated with respect. There are many sacred sites across Australia that are well documented within Aboriginal society. These are not respected by migaloo people because in most cases they have never bothered to ask about the significance of the sites to the traditional owners. If the significance is understood, then a political whitewash begins and some of these sites that can date back beyond fifty or sixty thousand years are lost forever.

Because we didn't create icons, or buildings to house our beliefs, the people who first invaded this land made the mistake of thinking there was nothing of spiritual value here. They couldn't see. What would the Italians think if visitors came in and knocked part of the Vatican down for a barbecue site, or if they put ladders inside the Sistine Chapel to get a closer look at Michelangelo's paintings of the Creation on the ceiling? Then why would you dig steel poles into Uluru so that hordes of tourists can walk all over this sacred place to get a better view? What kind of view does such disrespect give you?

I often think of religion and how it is good to be around people who believe in the same thing. You get strength from that. But in the early days, when we were swamped with Christianity and had the Bible shoved down our throats, the view that was taken was that Aboriginal people were heathens and needed to be saved. Thankfully, things are changing within the structure of the Christian church.

My mother says there is a lot of bitterness about the Christian church.

> They came here and totally disregarded our beliefs of the Creator who created all things. We didn't have Jesus but we had a lot of other beliefs. We have to acknowledge though, that in reality, we could have been wiped out if it wasn't for the churches. But now the church is changing. It is more accepting of Aboriginal traditions. Some churches invite our elders to do smoking ceremonies – our traditional way of cleansing – in the church. And many of the clergy talk about one God for all people now. Deacon Boniface Pridot, he's a tribal man from Daly River, he's in the Catholic church. He brings together the two beliefs so beautifully.

My dad sees the similarities between Aboriginal beliefs and Christianity. One example he gives is when visiting Bana Yelimaka, the sacred Medicine Waters of the Kung-gandji people. In order to call up its healing powers, before jumping in the water, you have to call out, 'Ngayu bana-kadai', and then the water bubbles up. For those who cannot speak the language they must first hit the water three times with a stick or branch before they step in. As my dad says, 'Well, that's not so different from acknowledging the Father, the Son and the Holy Ghost, is it?'

My mother has a very broad view of our beliefs.

You see, Aboriginal people are spiritual people. We will seek out that spirit, whatever form it takes. So, now, if Christianity is the thing, then we will go to this church or that church until we find where that spirituality really is for us. Spirituality is not so different, whatever your beliefs.

After all the tragedies that have happened in our family, my daughters say, 'Mum, you must change your mind about God.' But I don't. I think of the things I could have done to stop the tragedies happening. I look back and perhaps I knew there was something going wrong. I can't blame God for that. It was my own failings.

The things that you are not sure of, you can't act on at that time. It's only when you look back that you say, well, maybe I could have done some-thing. I can't blame God for that. He's been my strength. All the things he stands for, love for each other, the Truth and being responsible for your own actions, these are the things I believe in. I feel he is there all the time in my life. I don't know if this makes sense to anyone else.

By 'God' I mean the Creator through Aboriginal law. He made all things and he gave Aboriginal people the responsibility of the tribes. He gave them enough food and water but they had to work hard to get it. When they got up in the morning the first thing they did was to go out and hunt to fill their bellies up with food. The whole day might be spent gathering food. Nothing was wasted. They only hunted what they could eat. God was there for the Aboriginal people, otherwise they wouldn't be here today.

I see that same God in the Christian church. It's our same God, a caring God, that was always with our people. That's the way I feel about it. God is very important to all people. We should never lose sight of that, whatever happens.

My Aunty Val sums it up pretty well, I reckon. She says, 'The whitefullas were preaching to us what we were already practising, only they couldn't see that.'

I do a lot of work in Catholic schools. Every year I go to this very posh school and each time it comes to the dancing I ask the teachers to get up and dance, too. At that school they wear what I call Batman suits, those black capes; I think they call them academic gowns. I've got two to three hundred boys, Year 7s, 8s and 9s sitting on the floor in the hall. Everything is very strict. It is hard to make them laugh. I tried everything, some of my funniest lines and yet no one even smirked.

So, now it's time for the teachers to dance, and I yell out, 'Okay, you fullas, it's your turn. Take all those Batman capes off and get out here.' All the students just about broke their necks trying to look at their teachers to see what kind of reaction they would have. These fullas just threw off their capes, grabbed the branches and were out in the middle of the floor shaking their legs. That finally broke the ice and the boys started to relax and the room was filled with laughter. Phew!

I was having a chat to this young fulla who was taking me to the staffroom after the show. I asked him what he thought the highlight of the show was. He said, 'Father so-and-so smiling.' He said he had been there for a few years and this was the first time he'd seen Father smile.

I was invited back the year after. One of the teachers said that after my last visit, Father so-and-so was doing his usual Sunday morning service in the local church and this fly was buzzing around his face. Suddenly, he grabs this thing with the tassle on it and shakes his arms around like he's shaking the gum leaves in the Honey Dance to chase the black and yellow bees away. He goes, 'A aah, a aah, a aah, a aah.' He puts the tassel down and returns to the service he is conducting as if nothing happened!

My mum is right. The church is changing! She tells this great story about Father Mick.

A priest, Father Michael Peters, has played a big part in our lives in the last fifteen years or so. All the priests, the Jesuit priests especially, have helped us through a lot of tough patches. Father Mick has played a prominent role with all the Aboriginals on Palm Island and around here.

He went down to Toowoomba for an annual conference a few years back. They held a few different competitions for fun and to help people join in with each other – boomerang and spear throwing competitions and other things. People were at the conference from different parts of Australia, the Northern Territory and everywhere. Some good spear throwers were there, too. They had this banana palm and everyone was trying to spear the trunk.

Father Mick didn't fluke it. He speared that palm dead centre. He was the only one that hit it. He won the competition over all these Murris.

No one could believe it. We always laugh when migaloos try to do these things but not this time. He really jarred us up when he hit that trunk. I think he got a fright himself. We were all thinking in the back of our minds, 'He must have got some help from up above.'

After my brother Nick died, I found it very hard to sleep. I went back down to Tasmania where I was working at the Launceston Casino as a DJ. My brother Paul had given me Nick's didjeridoo and I kept it close to my bed and played it every night.

I remember resting the didj near the entrance to the bathroom before I went to bed early one morning after work. I had a horrific experience. I woke up screaming. It was a freezing cold night outside but my pyjamas and sheets were soaked with sweat. I started to shiver from the cold. I got up to go to the bathroom to have a hot shower and found the didjeridoo had moved from where I had put it when I went to bed. It was now in the corner. I showered and changed the sheets, and from that night on I was able to sleep.

The image of my brother Paul, lying in the back shed all twisted and broken with the rope around his neck, still haunts me. But for months and months after he hanged himself, I couldn't sleep. I was afraid to sleep. I didn't want to see him again like that. I tried everything. Sleeping pills, drugs, alcohol. None of them worked. Sometimes I would find myself curled up on the floor of the back shed sleeping where I last saw his body. These were the nights when I'd finished work DJing at two or three in the morning. I'd be in my suit and I'd stagger down to the back shed to be with him.

One night I staggered down the back. I was drunk and I'd decided I would join my brother. So I got this huge big tow rope. I could hardly lift it. It was for towing trucks and semitrailers, not for hanging blackfullas. Anyway, I tried to put it round my neck but I must have fallen on the floor. Probably decided it was too much hard work and I'd have a sleep and think about it tomorrow. That's how I woke up – lying on the floor with this huge tow rope on top of me. While recovering with my hangover, I thought of the headlines: 'Aboriginal man dies while trying to hang himself.' I could imagine Paul having a good laugh at me that night, too.

Things came to a head when I was in Sydney with my girlfriend. We had gone away on a holiday for a few days. This night I had this horrific vision where everything came at me. I thought I was going to die. I lifted up off the bed and screamed and screamed. She tried to hold me down. I didn't know what was going on.

Soon after I got back to my house in Melbourne, Weston Street, I was trying to sleep one night. I knew something was going to happen. I was on my stomach facing away from the door. I had a feeling that something else was in the room with me. I slowly turned my head towards the door.

I saw three figures standing there. They were all blackfullas. Budda Paul was in the middle. They were all painted up. My brother's hand came forward as he held it out to me. I didn't know whether he wanted me to come with him, or if he was saying he was okay. I just looked up at him and said, 'No, I'm okay, bros, I'm okay, Budda.' I put my head back on the pillow. When I looked up again, they were gone. After that night, I could sleep again.

My sister Kimmy hasn't come to me yet. Nor has my nephew Liam. I know they will come soon.

I know my brothers, my sister and my nephew are talking through me. I know why I'm still alive and I'm here now. There are lots of things that I am still learning from their passing. I think acknowledging the gift that I have as a communicator is a lot to do with their passing. I'm not scared of this gift any more and that's why this lightness is coming back to me.

That's why I keep on going. I keep doing this work in schools because it's my way of changing things, of making it better. I can see right there in front of me the face of a nation changing. I see it in the faces of these kids. They let you into their hearts and that's a nice place to be. They come into your heart as well. Just to remember a smile from a child or a hug from a teacher, like my good mate Vinny, that makes me feel warm. Also the echoes of strength that are in the voices of my parents, 'How you going, Mont? Just thought I'd ring up, see how you're going.' That keeps me sane and that protects me from being a lost spirit that's going to get hurt or that hurts itself.

The younger ones that are coming up now will be asking questions. Everybody has some skill or gift that they can use to help heal this country, young and old, black and white. I think my contribution is one link in the chain.

You see, we are all in the same boat. More to the point, we are all in the same land. When we die, we will all go back into the same earth. We Aboriginal people, we say, 'We don't own the land, the land owns us. When we die we go back to the earth. Our spirit will rest there. To belong here we must get to know this land. We must understand this place.'

It is for all of us who live here now to understand the land. Never ever forget where you come from. That is your strength. Your stories and your dances. Your culture. But remember where you are now. Find out about this place and the stories and dances, the culture that has been in this place for thousands and thousands of years, who knows how long? The Dreaming of this area is your Dreaming now because you were born here. This is your place, too.

If you don't learn about this place and love this land, then your spirit will be restless and you will feel like you don't belong. When your spirit is restless, that's when the racism and the bigotry comes in. Those are the people with restless spirits who don't love this place.

If we Aboriginals lose our spirituality, our culture, then you lose it, too. So we've got to work real fast before all the old people have gone, taking their stories and wisdom with them.

My people, when a baby is born, they have a ceremony called 'burning the baby'. They don't actually burn the baby but they hold the baby close to the fire so that it gets the warmth. The baby is passed around all the elders and they speak language to it and give it a birth name. My Aunty Val tells me the only one of us that this has happened to is my older sister Chrissy. Aunty said to me she saw her mother, Nanna Susie, sitting by the fire and warming her hands and rubbing little Chrissy all over as she spoke in Kunggandji language.

I'd been speaking to my cousin Bobby Patterson for years about Kunggandji people on Granny Jinnah Katchwan's side receiving a name. Finally, last Christmas it just happened.

Mum and Dad and Aunty Alma and I drove over to Uncle Herbert Patterson's place on Yarrabah. When we got out of the car, Aunty yelled out, 'Eh, Boori? You home, Boori?' She turned to me and said, 'That's his name. Boori. That mean fire.' I knew that 'boori' was fire but I never knew that was Uncle Herbert's name.

The others went off for a walk. I was sitting down talking to my uncle. We were talking about the getting of names. He just looked at me and said, 'You Boori. I give you my name. Boori means fire.' I sat there stunned. The place where we were was where the old people used to sit around the fire and tell the stories. I felt like that baby they were holding by the fire.

My mother and Aunty Alma were sitting over by the beach having a cup of tea. I could hardly walk over to them to tell them what had just happened.

I think in my case, having been away from my parents and Yarrabah and my mother's family for so long, for my uncle to give me his name, I felt very honoured. I felt like I'd earned his trust and respect to fight for and protect our people and to use any secrets he or my other uncles and aunties gave me wisely. This is the responsibility that comes with the gift to carry this name.

When your blackness is taken away from you and you feel unworthy of your culture, you are afraid to ask the elders for their knowledge because you feel like you don't have the right. On the other hand, they are waiting for you to ask. They think you're not interested because you don't ask and so they don't tell you. It's a vicious circle of silence.

My Aunty Val asked me why I didn't come to her for the stories. I said, 'Well, I didn't know that you had them.' My Aunty Val is the holder of lots of secrets. I never knew this until I was given my name. To be trusted and given these precious secrets is like being given a gift for all the hard years of struggle.

I suppose in a way it's like I've been through the initiation rights, but not the old way. My initiation was all of those deaths and how I dealt with them. I fought to get to that point where I am trusted to be given these things from the elders. If I have come through all these tests and I'm strong enough at the end to hold what the elders have to give, then here it is, here are the gifts.

In that moment of receiving my name I knew that it was for a reason that Budda Paul died at my place. I had to go through that. It was for a reason that I was the one to find his body on the ground. It made me strong. It almost killed me, but it made me strong.

Knowledge is passed on to those who are strong enough to keep it. The elders have to see that strength in you to know that you can keep the secrets and hold the knowledge. You have to be interested not just

197

through seeing with your eyes or hearing with your ears because that means it can go in one ear and out the other. Most importantly, your heart must be open and free because it is only when all three are one – the eyes, the ears and the heart – that stories and secrets and songs can be given in trust.

When my uncle gave me my name, I felt like I belonged to myself. Nobody could take anything away from me now. Nothing or nobody can hurt or kill my spirit even if they take a gun in their hand and pull the trigger. I know my spirit will stay strong. The bullet might take my life but nothing else.

--≈⊃⊂⊂∰

I used to think my Aunty Val was all churchy and I never knew that she would know so much about our stories and secrets. To most people, if they saw Aunty Val walking down the street they would never imagine one jot of what she knows. She phoned me up not long after I got my name and said I should come over, she had stories to give me. It took me a week to go around. I had sleepless nights. I was afraid. Even though I felt strong within myself and I had my name, I was wondering if I would have the power to hold what she had to give me.

When I went around she was very matter of fact. She just said, 'Don't worry about that, you have.' She looked into my eyes and I suppose she could see that what she wanted to pass on was safe with me. She can see that I have never gone after money or brushed aside where I am from and who I am.

I remember in this one school a kid saying, 'What if someone paid you a million dollars to do a dance that you weren't s'posed to do in front of us?' I said, 'Well, I wouldn't do it.' He said, 'What if it was two million?' I said, 'I still wouldn't.' 'What if was a billion?' 'I still wouldn't.' 'What about a zillion?' He was about to go on adding more dollars signs when I interrupted and said, 'Hold on. That's your value. That's not ours. Your value is the dollar sign. Our value is respecting what has been passed on. What you offer is paper money. What we value is totally different.'

I wouldn't do that because it is against my spirit. You are only here X amount of years as you are, as flesh and bone, but your spirit is the thing that's inside and there forever.

Now my Aunty Val is giving me lots of things. She tells me lots of things that I have to go away and digest. Even when we talk sometimes I have to get up and go outside. My heart pounds and I have to rest before I can take any more.

I always thought Nanna Susie, my grandmother, couldn't speak our language, because I remember spending lots of time with her as a child. I don't remember her speaking language once. My aunty tells me stories now of Nanna Susie speaking it fluently to her mother, Granny Jinnah. When I asked why she never taught any of us this language, Aunty Val says, 'A lot of their journey is very

199

hurtful. A lot of the old people don't talk about what has happened for the simple reason that it hurts too much. What they have seen hurts too much. So we stay quiet.'

I know the stories about what white law did to try and stamp out our language but I didn't realise the depth of pain there that would stop a grandmother teaching her grandchildren.

I want to spend a lot of time with my Aunty Val now.

This German woman and I were having a conversation about Aboriginal people in Australia. She was asking me all sorts of questions about spiritual beliefs, customs, art, anything and everything you could want to know about blackfullas in this country. She showed me a book she was reading and spoke strongly about the atrocities she had read about and asked me if in the near future there are any chances of these issues being addressed. I explained what I am trying to do, what my family is try-ing to do, and what my people are trying to do to change things. Then she asked this question, 'What do you think white people have given Aboriginal people that's good?' I didn't have an answer. She looked at me and said, 'The written word? How about the power to write?'

Maybe tomorrow
all our eyes ears and hearts will be as one
then nunjull the sun
can shine to warm even the darkest thought
Maybe tomorrow
then in this warm light the earth will be seen
her beauty and power felt
her tales of creation heard
through story rocks and sacred waters
Maybe tomorrow
we will not mine, dig and sift
for the gift
the earth our mother has to give us
Maybe tomorrow
the keepers of her secrets will be heard
word for word
then our journey can begin together
our dusty mother will give way
as we walk and talk
to retrace the footsteps of time itself
then
Maybe tomorrow
we will all sit in the circle of life
same rhythm
same time

My nephews on the beach at Yarrabah
*It's the strength I get from Yarrabah that makes me able to get
up and communicate with audiences of white people.*

ACKNOWLEDGEMENTS

There are many people to thank for this book.

Thanks to my mother and father, who are always there for me, no matter what. To all my aunties and uncles and my Nanna Susie who, along with my mum and dad, installed in my mind and heart the way of my people – 'we not me'.

To my sisters, Mimby, Cilla, Sue, Toni, Chubby, Chicky, Chrissy and brothers, Nick, Paul and Rocky. Although some are gone we are still one big strong family.

To all my nieces and nephews, and my cousins, the Pryor mob from Birri-gubba Nation and the Stell mob from the Kunggandji Nation.

To Margaret Dunkle, who watched over the writing of this book. With her love and dear friendship I felt strong and confident within myself. Thank you, dear Margaret.

To Meme McDonald. Without this wonderful person, this book would not have been. She kicked my backside when it needed kicking, picked me up when I almost fell, saw the beauty and strength of my family. She was able to capture them in pictures and helped to use words to shape images of my people that moved some of the dark clouds that have hovered for too long. She is in the hearts of my family, especially in mine. Meme – thank you.

To Jojo Girragundji Lovell and Grace Cockatoo Lovell, Mari and Ciaran, Sonia Borg, Camilla Fligelman for her patience and understanding, and to Jimmi George, Lena, Mere and Toto from the Curlewis St, Bondi Blackpackers. To Glen Leitch, Young Australia Workshop – thank you for your help through tough times and, more importantly, for your understanding and friendship. To the Brady Bunch – Vincent, Graham, William and Matthew – for your strength.

To Erica Irving. On a freezing Saturday morning at five-thirty after a Wurundjeri Welcoming, we walked along the banks of the Yarra and talked about the book. I saw the light shining from you. Thank you, Erica, for seeing my people's dream.

To Karin Riederer, and everyone at Penguin. Nelia, Maria, Michael and Marissa and Julia Messner, Glenda Davis, Juliet Bradford and Lakaya, Maggie Urban and Jaii, Miss Green, my Maths teacher at Pimlico High, my sporting coaches, Libby Gregory, Linda Waters, Carol and Ruby Ruff, Larry and Lou-Ann Holmes, Ramona Singh, Rachel, Malcolm Jack and Eve Schonheimer, Patrick Dromé, Lance Reiley and family, and Joy Murphy.

To the Aboriginal Arts Board of the Australia Council for their assistance in writing this book.

To every single school or institution that I have performed in or spoken to from pre-school to Year 12. Without your learning eyes, loving hearts and listening ears this book would not be, and probably, neither would I. I thank you all.

Boori

When I first went to Yarrabah and walked the land that Boori's people had walked for thousands of years, I felt very sad for what we migaloos had missed out on. The privilege of writing this book with Boori has taken away a lot of that sorrow and replaced it with a treasure box of experiences. My eyes and my heart have been opened to see this country, my home, in a new way. My children will grow up with this understanding – thank you, Boori, for this gift.

I am so grateful to the Pryor family for making me welcome, for being so patient with my endless questions and for trusting me with precious stories and photographs.

Also, thanks to Chris, Joe and Grace and my sister, Libby, for their love and support, and to the many dear friends who have been so enthusiastic about the writing of this book. A special thank you to two great photographers, Robert Colvin and Naomi Herzog, who gave their advice, guidance and loan of equipment so generously at any hour of the day or night. Thanks also to my agent, Jenny Darling, and Jacinta Dimase.

Meme